your guide to
energy-saving
home
improvements

your guide to energy-saving home improvements

GROSSET & DUNLAP
A FILMWAYS COMPANY
Publishers • New York

Acknowledgements

This manual has been prepared by Abt Associates Inc. for the Division of Energy, Building Technology and Standards, Office of Policy Development and Research, U.S. Department of Housing and Urban Development.

The authors wish to thank Mr. Robert C. Jones, Jr. AIA, from the Division of Energy, Building Technology and Standards at HUD, for his untiring professional assistance and support. His concern that this manual be a useful and convenient tool for homeowners has guided us throughout the course of this project.

This document was reviewed by an Advisory Committee of the American Society of Heating, Refrigerating and Air Conditioning Engineers, Inc. (ASHRAE) for general consistency with current good practice for modification of existing housing to reduce energy use. At review meetings and informal discussions, valuable constructive dialogue between the members of the Committee and the authors has greatly assisted in the resolution of many of the technical issues dealt with in this manual. The members of the Review Committee were: Charles P. Robart, Jr., Chairman, Tamami Kusuda, Ph.D., and William Rudoy, Ph.D.

The authors wish to thank the following organizations, who by their assistance have made substantive contribution to the content and quality of this publication:

The National Bureau of Standards, for the assistance from the Center for Building Technology, in the technical and editorial review of the final drafts.

The Federal Energy Administration, for the constructive comments from their Building Branch on the final draft.

Hittman Associates, Inc. whose scientific work in the field of residential energy conservation provided a starting point for our efforts.

The Reader's Digest, Inc. who kindly gave their permission to reference their illustrations in the preparation of some of the graphic work.

The American Gas Association; The Association of Home Appliance Manufacturers; Boston Edison Company; Boston Gas; The Brick Institute of America; Certain-Teed Products Corporation; The Davenport Insulation Company; Florida Power Corporation; HC Products Company; Honeywell, Inc.; The Illinois Power Company; Johns-Manville Corporation; Michigan Consolidated Gas Company; The National Association of Home Builders and the NAHB Research Foundation, Inc.; Owens-Corning Fiberglas Corporation; The National Environmental Systems Contractors Association; Sears, Roebuck and Company; W.R. Grace and Company.

Authors

Principal Authors:

Allan D. Ackerman, Project Manager
Bryan J. Burke
Peter T. Hogarth

Project Staff:

David J. MacFadyen, Project Director
Deborah Blackwell
Robert F. Stone
Roy P. Nelson
Linda M. Wurm
Margaret Bucciero

Consultants:

James R. Simpson
Michael E. Brose
Steven Nelson

Disclaimer

Introduction

Homeowners no longer need to be told that heating and cooling costs are taking a much bigger bite out of their budget than ever before. The energy pinch is still on and threatens to grow more severe each year. Many people have searched for one reliable source of readily understandable information on energy saving home improvements, but have been unable to locate any such source.

This guide is the result of extensive research and several surveys of existing house construction types. Energy saving techniques applicable to those types were gathered and compared as. to cost and potential fuel savings. The comparison was designed to emphasize safe and cost-saving energy conservation techniques that would return the greatest practical net savings to the homeowner over the life of the investment.

Step-by-step installation instructions for each project are combined with clear illustrations that take the mystery out of seemingly complex tasks. The reader is instructed in the fine arts of caulking, weatherstripping, insulating, and installing storm doors and windows so that he or she can confidently seal out the elements while retaining maximum heating or cooling in the home. The answers are all here for your home, wherever it is in the country. Some of the projects to save energy will cost you some money to install, but many of them are absolutely free.

By fixing up your home, you win in a lot of ways: you use less energy and save money year after year, you add resale value to your home, and you make a sound investment in your home. We believe this manual can help you save dollars in home energy expenditures and we invite you to begin one or more of these projects today.

CONTENTS

PART 1: A QUICK LOOK AT YOUR HOME

PART 1: A QUICK LOOK AT YOUR HOME

There are ranges of costs and saving given for the energy-saving home improvements below. Where your house falls in that range depends on the size and type of your house, the climate in your area, and what you pay for fuel. For purposes of comparison, a single-story, 1250-square-foot home in these cities will fall at about the midpoint of the range:

Packages 1 & 2 (Natural Gas Heat)	Package 3 (Electric Air-conditioning)
Washington, D.C.	Washington, D.C.
Youngstown, Ohio	Cairo, Ill.
Shreveport, La.	Atlanta, Ga.
Eureka, Calif.	Oklahoma City, Okla.
	Bakersfield, Calif.

YOUR HEATING SAVINGS

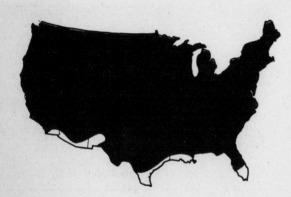

You can save significantly on heating if you live practically anywhere in the U.S.A.

Look at the map above.

If you live in the part of the country that's shaded, here are two packages of energy-saving measures for you:

Package 1 is cheap and easy, and it pays for itself every year.

Package 2 saves even more, year after year. It can cut your heating bills by as much as one-half. It will pay for itself within 5 years.

Package 1

1. Turn thermostat down 6° in winter from your usual setting.

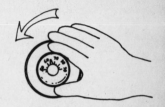

Package 2

1. Turn thermostat down 6° in winter from your usual setting.

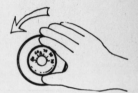

3. Service your oil furnace.

IF YOU HAVE WHOLE-HOUSE AIR-CONDITIONING

Package 3

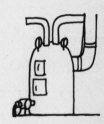

Here's the package of energy-saving measures for you.

Look at the map to the left.

Package 3 can save you money on your air-conditioning bills if you live in the shaded portion of the country.

2. Put on plastic storm windows.

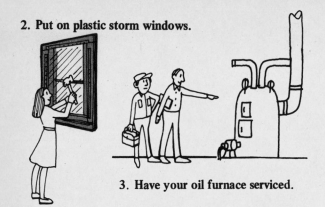

3. Have your oil furnace serviced.

Here's an idea of what **Package 1** costs and saves in a typical home.

	Yearly Cost	Yearly Savings
1. turn down thermostat	$0	$20-65
2. put on plastic storms	$5-7	$20-55
3. service oil furnace	$25	$25-65
TOTAL	**$30-32**	**$65-185**

— If you already have storm windows, or if you don't have an oil furnace — then take a look at package 2.

---

2. Put on plastic storm windows.

5. Insulate your attic.

4. Caulk and weatherstrip your doors and windows.

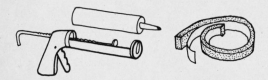

Here's an idea of what **Package 2** costs and saves in a typical home (Items 4 and 5 reduce the heating bill to which the effects of Items 1, 2, and 3 are applied, so 1, 2, and 3 save less here than in Package 1):

	1st Year Cost	Yearly Savings
1. turn down thermostat	$0	$10-40
2. put on plastic storms	$5-7	$15-45
3. service oil furnace	$25	$15-40
4. caulk and weatherstrip	$75-105*	$30-75
5. insulate attic	$160-290*	$35-120
TOTAL	**$265-427**	**$105-320**

* These are do-it-yourself costs. If you called a contractor, these items could cost twice as much.

You might or might not need to do all of these things. Turn the page to find out which items apply to your home.

---

1. Turn thermostat up 6° in summer from your usual setting.

2. Insulate your attic.

3. Caulk and weatherstrip your doors and windows.

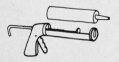

Here's an idea of what **Package 3** costs and saves in a typical home:

	1st Year Cost	Yearly Savings
1. turn up thermostat	$0	$5-15
2. insulate attic	$160-290*	$25-50
3. caulk and weatherstrip	$75-105*	$20-50
TOTAL	**$235-395**	**$50-115**

* These are do-it-yourself costs. If you called a contractor, these items could cost twice as much.

You might or might not need to do all of these things. Turn the page to find out which items apply to your home.

And if you live in the part of the country that's shaded on both maps, these cooling savings are *in addition* to what you save on heating — turn the page to see what your total savings will be.

3

HEATING AND AIR-CONDITIONING SAVINGS TOGETHER

If you have whole-house air conditioning and if you live in the part of the country that's shaded on **both** of the maps on the previous page, some of the energy-saving steps save on **both** heating and cooling — but you only have to pay for them once.

LOOK AT THESE TWO TABLES FOR AN ESTIMATE OF THE COMBINED COSTS AND SAVINGS FOR A TYPICAL HOME:

Package 1 plus turning up the thermostat in summer:

	Yearly Cost	Yearly Savings
turn thermostat lower in winter	$0	$20-65
turn thermostat higher in summer	$0	$5-15
put on plastic storms	$5-7	$20-55
service oil furnace	$25	$25-65
TOTAL	$30-32	$70-200

Package 2 and Package 3 together:

	1st Year Cost	Yearly Savings
turn down thermostat in winter	$0	$20-65
turn up thermostat in summer	$0	$5-15
put on plastic storms	$5-7	$15-55
service oil furnace	$25	$15-40
caulk and weatherstrip	$75-105*	$50-125
insulate attic	$160-290*	$60-170
TOTAL	$265-427	$170-470

* These are do-it-yourself costs. If you have a contractor do it, these items could cost about twice as much.

Which items do you need to do?

Everyone can profit from turning their thermostat down in winter and up in summer.

If you live in the part of the country that's shaded on the large map on the last page (and nearly everyone does), you should:

Put on storm windows if you don't have them already. Plastic ones are cheapest. See page 38.

Service your oil furnace each year if you have one. See page 61. If you have a gas furnace, service it every three years and save, too.

Whether or not you need weatherstripping and caulking, or attic insulation, depends on what your house is like. Here's how to tell whether you need them:

Do you need caulking or putty?

Look around the edges of a typical window, where the picture shows. Check the edges of your doors, too. There should be some filler in all these cracks. That's either *caulking* or *putty*. If it's old, brittle, and broken up, or if it's missing altogether, you need to put some in. Go to page 32 to find out how to do it.

Do you need weatherstripping?

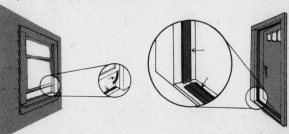

Look for the strips of vinyl, metal, or foam rubber around the edges of your windows and doors. That's *weatherstripping*. If it's missing or deteriorated, you need to put some in. Go to pages 34-37 to find out how to do it.

Do you need attic insulation?

Go up into your attic and see how much insulation is there. Usually, there's a door or hatchway to the attic. If not, get a contractor to check it for you. Look at the table on page 42 to see how much more insulation you need.

PART 2: A CLOSER LOOK AT YOUR HOME

PART 2: A CLOSER LOOK AT YOUR HOME

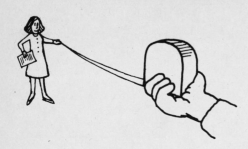

This part of your manual takes a closer look at your home, where it is in the country, and the best, cheapest way to fix up your house to save energy. In Part 2 there are 12 valuable energy-saving steps. You'll find out which ones apply to your home and:

1. **How much they'll cost;** of those steps that do apply, which you can afford.

2. **Which to do first;** of those steps you can afford, which ones get you your money back the fastest.

3. **How much you'll save** by taking an energy-saving step.

You Can Skip Some of Part 2

Each energy-saving step has a page or two in this part. Go through these one at a time. You'll see immediately that you can skip some of them.

There's a section at the beginning of the pages on each energy-saving step. Reading this section and checking some items around your home, you'll find some more measures you can skip.

Some of Part 2 is Just What You Need

There are sure to be several energy-saving steps here that *do* apply to your home. Every time you find a step that does, follow the pages through until you get the two important numbers for each step: COST, and SAVINGS FACTOR, then copy them onto the Energy Checklist at the end of the book. The Energy Checklist lets you see all the numbers for your energy-saving steps in one place. Once you've copied your COST and SAVINGS FACTOR onto the Checklist, there's a little arithmetic — the directions are all right there. Then you're ready to go — you'll know what to do first, how much you'll save the first year, and whether you can afford it.

CAULK AND WEATHERSTRIP YOUR DOORS AND WINDOWS

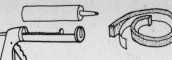

Caulking and weatherstripping are good cheap ways to save energy. It's worth your while to check to see if you need caulking, putty, or weatherstripping on your windows and doors.

DO THEY NEED CAULKING OR PUTTY?

Look at a typical window and a typical door. Look at the parts shown in the pictures. Check the box next to the description that best fits what you see:

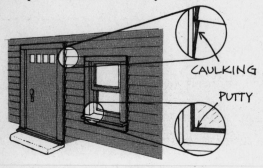

CAULKING

PUTTY

☐ OK . . . All the cracks are completely filled with caulking. The putty around the window panes is solid and unbroken; no drafts.

☐ FAIR . . . The caulking and putty are old and cracked, or missing in places; minor drafts.

☐ POOR . . . There's no caulking at all. The putty is in poor condition; noticeable drafts.

If you checked either "FAIR" or "POOR", then you probably need caulking.

DO THEY NEED WEATHERSTRIPPING?

A. YOUR WINDOWS

Look at the parts shown in the pictures of one or two of your typical windows. Check one:

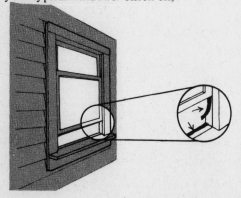

☐ OK . . . Good, unbroken weatherstripping in all the indicated places; no drafts.

☐ FAIR . . . Weatherstripping damaged or missing in places; minor drafts.

☐ POOR . . . No weatherstripping at all; noticeable drafts.

If you checked either "FAIR" or "POOR", then your windows probably need weatherstripping.

B. YOUR DOORS

Look at the parts of your doors shown in the picture. Check one:

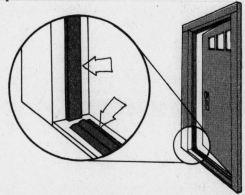

☐ OK . . . Good, unbroken weatherstripping in all the indicated places; no drafts.

☐ FAIR . . . Weatherstripping damaged or missing in places; minor drafts.

☐ POOR . . . No weatherstripping at all; noticeable drafts.

If you checked either "FAIR" or "POOR", then your doors probably need weatherstripping.

IF YOU CHECKED "OK" FOR ALL ITEMS, THEN YOU DON'T NEED CAULKING, PUTTY, OR WEATHERSTRIPPING. GO ON TO PAGE 10

IF YOU CHECKED "FAIR" OR "POOR" FOR ANY ITEM, COMPLETE THE NEXT PAGE.

Find Your Cost

1. Multiply the number of windows that need *caulking and putty* times the cost per window: ——→ [number of windows] X $2.90 = [   ]

2. Multiply the number of windows that need *weatherstripping* times the cost per window: ——→ [number of windows] X $2.00 = [   ]

3. Multiply the number of doors that need *caulking* times the cost per door: ——→ [number of doors] X $2.75 = [   ]

4. Multiply the number of doors that need *weatherstripping* times the cost per door: ——→ [number of doors] X $6.00 = [   ]

5. Add up these numbers to get the total: ——→ TOTAL COST $ [   ]

This cost is your estimated *do-it-yourself* cost. (It's easy to do yourself — look at **page 32**.) If you get a contractor to do it, your costs will be greater — at least 2 to 4 times as much. Prices vary from area to area and from job to job, so check with local contractors for an estimate (see page 64).

Find Your Savings Factor

Fill out only the lines that apply to your house:

A. YOUR WINDOWS

caulking and putty:

in FAIR condition: ——————→ [number of windows] X 0.3 = [   ]

in POOR condition: ——————→ [number of windows] X 1.0 = [   ]

weatherstripping:

in FAIR condition: ——————→ [number of windows] X 1.0 = [   ]

in POOR condition: ——————→ [number of windows] X 8.4 = [   ]

Multiply these two numbers

B. YOUR DOORS

caulking:

in FAIR condition: ——————→ [number of doors] X 0.3 = [   ]

in POOR condition: ——————→ [number of doors] X 0.9 = [   ]

weatherstripping:

in FAIR condition: ——————→ [number of doors] X 2.0 = [   ]

in POOR condition: ——————→ [number of doors] X 16.8 = [   ]

Multiply these two numbers

C. Add up all the numbers you've written in the boxes to the right and write the total here: This number is your savings factor. ——————→ SAVINGS FACTOR [   ]

GO TO THE ENERGY CHECKLIST AT THE END OF THE BOOK

Write the *total cost* you found above in the cost box on line 1 of the Checklist.

Write the *savings factor* you found above in the savings box on line 1 of the Checklist.

INSTALL STORM WINDOWS

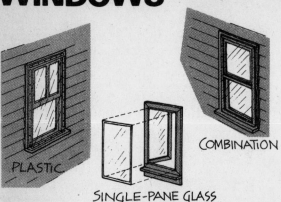

PLASTIC

SINGLE-PANE GLASS

COMBINATION

There are three kinds of storm windows:

PLASTIC. These cost only 50¢ each. You may have to put up replacements each year.

SINGLE PANE GLASS. They cost about $10.00 each. You put them up and take them down each year.

TRIPLE-TRACK GLASS (COMBINATION). These have screens and you can open and close them. They are for double-hung windows only (like the one in the picture). They cost about $30.00 each installed. Double-track storm windows are also available, and they cost less.

All three kinds are about equally effective. The more expensive ones are more attractive and convenient.

FILL OUT ONE OR MORE OF LINES A, B, AND C — WHICHEVER ONES YOU'RE INTERESTED IN.

A. PUT ON PLASTIC STORM WINDOWS WITHOUT WEATHERSTRIPPING

Your cost: Count the number of windows you have and multiply times $.50:

_____ X $.50 = $ [   ]
number of windows   total cost

Your Savings: In step A on page 8 you checked either "OK," "fair," or "poor" as the condition of the weatherstripping on your windows.

- If you checked "OK",
  circle this number   **7.9**
- If you checked "FAIR"
  circle this number   **8.2**
- If you checked "POOR"
  circle this number   **10.8**

Multiply the number you circled times the number of windows you have:

_____ X _____ = [   ]
number you   number of   savings factor
circled   windows

B. PUT ON PLASTIC STORM WINDOWS AT THE SAME TIME YOU WEATHERSTRIP
(see Note)

Your cost: Multiply your number of windows times $.50:

_____ X $.50 = $ [   ]
number of windows   total cost

Your savings: Multiply your number of windows times 7.9 :

_____ X 7.9 = [   ]
number of windows   savings factor

C. PUT ON GLASS STORM WINDOWS
(see Note)

Your cost: Choose which kind of glass storm windows you want.

- If you want single pane windows, multiply the number of windows you have times $10.00 (do-it-yourself installation):
- For combination windows, multiply the number of windows you have times $30.00 (includes installation):

_____ X $ _____ = $ [   ]
number of windows $10 or $30   total cost

Your savings: Multiply your number of windows times 7.9 :

_____ X 7.9 = [   ]
number of windows   savings factor

SEE THE ENERGY CHECKLIST AT THE END OF THE BOOK

NOTE: These cost and savings factors are for storm windows only. They are in addition to the costs and savings for caulking and weatherstripping that you found on the last page.

If you filled out Part A here, fill out line 2a of the Checklist.

If you filled out Part B here, fill out line 2b of the Checklist.

If you filled out Part C here, fill out line 2c of the Checklist.

In each case, write the total cost into the cost box on that line and the savings factor into the savings box.

INSULATING YOUR ATTIC

Attic insulation is one of the most important energy-saving home improvements you can make. This section talks about insulating 3 kinds of attics.

IF YOUR HOME HAS ONE OF THE 3 KINDS SHOWN BELOW,

go straight to the page in this section that applies, work it through, and fill out one of the lines in the attic portion of the Energy Checklist at the end of the book.

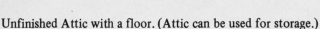

Unfinished Attics

Unfinished Attic without a floor. (Attic isn't used at all): (this includes Attics with roof trusses in them.)

Page 12

Unfinished Attic with a floor. (Attic can be used for storage.)

Page 14

Finished Attics

Finished Attic that can be used for living or storage.

Page 16

IF YOUR HOME IS A COMBINATION OF TWO KINDS OF ATTICS

(part of your attic may be finished and heated, part may be unused except as storage, as in these sample houses):

If this is your situation, treat each of your attics separately. Go to both of the pages in this section that apply, and fill out both lines in the attic portion of the Energy Checklist at the end of the book.

FINISHED ATTIC

UNFINISHED, UNFLOORED ATTIC

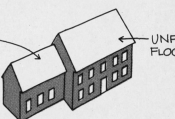

UNFINISHED, FLOORED ATTIC

Flat roof? Mansard roof?

If your home has a flat roof, or a mansard roof, it will be harder and more expensive to insulate than the others — talk to a contractor — see Part 3 on how to pick a contractor.

 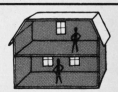

INSULATE YOUR UNFINISHED ATTIC

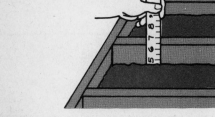

This is the kind of attic you have if it has no floor — at most some loose boards to walk on, and you don't ever plan to finish it.

Should you insulate it?

It depends on how much insulation is already there. To find out, go up into your attic and measure the depth of the insulation.

NO

If you already have 6" or more, you may have enough, and you can skip the rest of this page. Check the table on page 42 to be sure.

Yes

If you have less than 6", you may need more, and you should keep going on this page. Start by writing down the approximate thickness you have:

_____ inches

You'll need this number in a minute.

Go on to the next column.

NOTE: If you can't get up into your attic to measure your insulation, you will need a contractor to do the work. Call him for a cost estimate. Ask the contractor to tell you how much insulation is already there along with an estimate for "R-19" insulation.

LESS THAN SIX INCHES?
Go through the steps marked 1 and 2 on this and the next page. Then read the directions in the lower right-hand corner of the next page to interpret the chart.

1. Should you do-it-yourself or hire a contractor?

You can do-it-yourself if there's a way for you to get up into the attic and if you're willing to do about a day's work.

If you aren't sure whether you want to do-it-yourself, look at page 45 of the manual to help you decide.

Check "do-it-yourself" or "contractor" in one of the boxes below.

IF YOU DON'T HAVE ANY INSULATION AT ALL,

YOU NEED THIS KIND OF INSULATION*

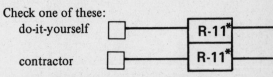

Check one of these:
do-it-yourself ☐ — R-22*
contractor ☐ — R-22*

IF YOU HAVE UNDER 2 INCHES,

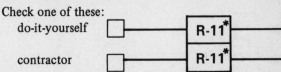

Check one of these:
do-it-yourself ☐ — R-11*
contractor ☐ — R-11*

IF YOU HAVE FROM 2 TO 4 INCHES,

Check one of these:
do-it-yourself ☐ — R-11*
contractor ☐ — R-11*

IF YOU HAVE FROM 4 TO 6 INCHES,

It will be economical to add another 3½ inches if you have electric heat and live in a cold part of the country.*

2. How big is your attic?

To get your attic area, you don't even have to go up into the attic. Find out the area of the first floor of your home, not counting the garage, porch, and other unheated areas, and it will be the same as the area of your attic.

If it's a rectangle:

Measure its length and width in feet to the nearest foot and multiply them together.

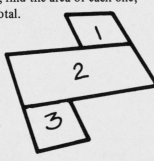

If it's a combination:

Break it down into rectangles, find the area of each one, then add the areas to get the total.

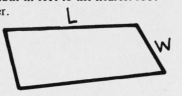

length   X   width   =   area

_____ X _____ = _____

length   X   width   =   area

1 _____ X _____ = _____

2 _____ X _____ = _____

3 _____ X _____ = _____

total area _____

Check the number of square feet below that's closest to your total attic area

	600 Sq. Ft. ☐	900 Sq. Ft. ☐	1200 Sq. Ft. ☐	1600 Sq. Ft. ☐	2000 Sq. Ft. ☐
Cost	$108	$162	$216	$288	$360
Savings Factor	236	355	473	630	788
Cost	$180	$270	$360	$480	$600
Savings Factor	236	355	473	630	788

Read across and down the chart from the boxes you've checked to find which square in the chart applies to you, like this:

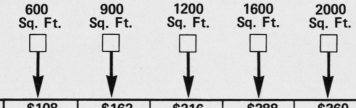

	600 Sq. Ft.	900 Sq. Ft.	1200 Sq. Ft.	1600 Sq. Ft.	2000 Sq. Ft.
Cost	$54	$81	$108	$144	$180
Savings Factor	51	77	102	136	170
Cost	$114	$171	$288	$304	$380
Savings Factor	51	77	102	136	170

Copy these two numbers onto line 3 of the Energy Checklist at the end of the book. The top number, your cost, goes in the cost box, the bottom number, your savings factor, goes in the savings box.

	600 Sq. Ft.	900 Sq. Ft.	1200 Sq. Ft.	1600 Sq. Ft.	2000 Sq. Ft.
Cost	$54	$81	$108	$144	$180
Savings Factor	22	33	44	59	74
Cost	$114	$171	$228	$304	$380
Savings Factor	22	33	44	59	74

*In some cases, it may be economical to add even more — see page 42.

INSULATE YOUR UNFINISHED FLOORED ATTIC

This is your kind of attic if it's unfinished and unheated but has a floor.

Should you insulate it?

It depends on how much insulation is already there. To find out, go up there and check.

The insulation, if there is any, will be in either of two places:

Between the rafters. The first place to look is up between the rafters and in the walls at the ends of the attic.

Under the floor. If it's not up between the rafters, it might be down under the floorboards. If so, it won't be easy to see. You'll have to look around the edges of the attic, or through any large cracks in the floor. A flashlight may be handy, and also a ruler or stick that you can poke through the cracks with. If there's any soft, fluffy material in there, that's insulation.

Wherever the insulation is, if it's there at all, estimate how thick it is.

No

If it's thicker than 4 inches, it's not economical to add more — skip the rest of this page.

Yes

If it's 4 inches thick or less, you might need more — fill out these two pages to help you decide.

NOTE: **If you can't tell whether you have enough insulation up there, get a contractor to find out for you. You're likely to be calling one anyway to do the work, and you'll want a cost estimate from him. Ask the contractor to tell you how much insulation is already there, and use the figures he gives you to complete this page and fill out the Energy Checklist.**

Your cost and savings

To get a quick estimate of your costs and savings, follow steps 1 and 2 below and on the next page.

1. Which method?

There are two basic ways to insulate this type of attic.

a. Insulate the rafters, end walls, and collar beams.

This is the best way if you're doing it yourself, or if you think you might ever finish the attic.

b. The other way is to blow loose insulation in under the attic floor. This is a contractor job — you can't do it yourself. Also, don't do this if you think you might ever finish the attic. But if you're going to call a contractor, this is the cheapest and most effective way.

To see what's involved in a do-it-yourself job of insulating the rafters, end walls, and collar beams, look at page 49. What's involved when a contractor does the work is on page 48.

There are three different methods listed below. Pick the one that you think you might want to do. For the method you've chosen, check one of the three boxes — the *top* one if there's no existing insulation, the *middle* one if there's up to 2 inches of existing insulation, or the *bottom* one if there's from 2 to 4 inches of existing insulation.

Then go to step 2 on the next page.

DO-IT-YOURSELF: RAFTERS, END WALLS, COLLAR BEAMS

No existing insulation ☐

0-2 inches ☐

2-4 inches ☐

CONTRACTOR INSTALLATION: RAFTERS, END WALLS, COLLAR BEAMS

No existing insulation ☐

0-2 inches ☐

2-4 inches ☐

CONTRACTOR INSTALLATION: UNDER ATTIC FLOOR

No existing insulation ☐

0-2 inches ☐

2-4 inches ☐

2. How big is your attic?

Your unfinished, floored attic area will be either shaped like a rectangle or a combination of rectangles.

If it's a rectangle:

Measure it's length and width in feet to the nearest foot and multiply them together.

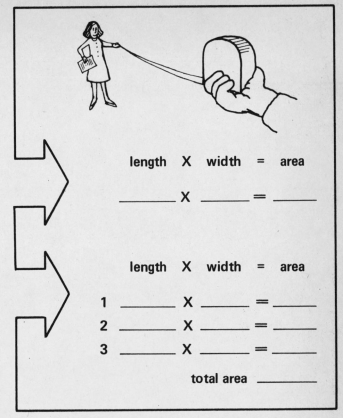

length X width = area

_____ X _____ = _____

If it's a combination:

Break it down into rectangles, find the area of each one, then add the areas to get the total.

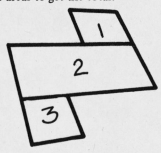

length X width = area

1 _____ X _____ = _____

2 _____ X _____ = _____

3 _____ X _____ = _____

total area _____

Check the number of square feet below that's closest to your attic floor area:

	600 Sq. Ft.	900 Sq. Ft.	1200 Sq. Ft.	1600 Sq. Ft.	2000 Sq. Ft.
Cost / Savings Factor	$130 / 83	$190 / 121	$245 / 165	$315 / 224	$385 / 284
Cost / Savings Factor	$105 / 27	$160 / 41	$205 / 57	$275 / 74	$340 / 92
Cost / Savings Factor	$90 / 11	$135 / 18	$175 / 25	$230 / 34	$285 / 43

	600 Sq. Ft.	900 Sq. Ft.	1200 Sq. Ft.	1600 Sq. Ft.	2000 Sq. Ft.
Cost / Savings Factor	$240 / 83	$360 / 121	$480 / 165	$640 / 224	$800 / 284
Cost / Savings Factor	$210 / 27	$315 / 41	$420 / 55	$560 / 72	$700 / 88
Cost / Savings Factor	$180 / 9	$270 / 15	$360 / 22	$480 / 30	$600 / 38

	600 Sq. Ft.	900 Sq. Ft.	1200 Sq. Ft.	1600 Sq. Ft.	2000 Sq. Ft.
Cost / Savings Factor	$265 / 101	$385 / 151	$500 / 202	$645 / 269	$785 / 336
Cost / Savings Factor	$235 / 37	$345 / 56	$450 / 74	$570 / 99	$725 / 124
Cost / Savings Factor	$210 / 14	$305 / 21	$400 / 28	$520 / 37	$635 / 46

How to read the chart

Read down and across from the boxes you've checked to find which square in the chart applies to you, like this:

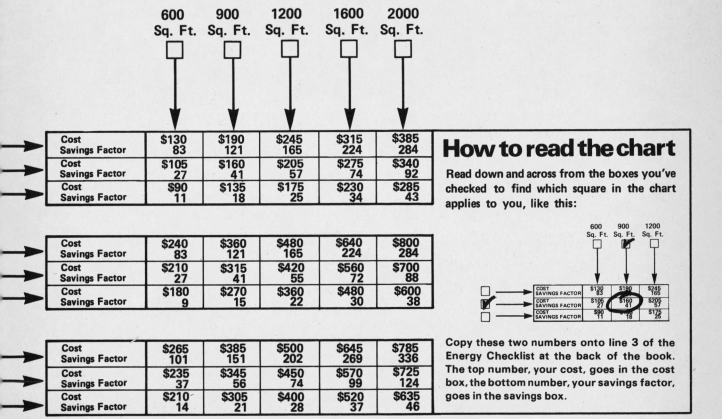

Copy these two numbers onto line 3 of the Energy Checklist at the back of the book. The top number, your cost, goes in the cost box, the bottom number, your savings factor, goes in the savings box.

INSULATE YOUR FINISHED ATTIC

This attic is a little harder to insulate than an unfinished attic because some parts are hard to reach. A contractor can do a complete job, but if you do-it-yourself, there will probably be parts that you can't reach.

Should you insulate it?

You need to find out if there's enough insulation there already.

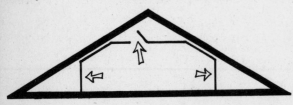

Depending on what your house is like, you may or may not be able to measure your insulation by getting into the unfinished spaces in your attic through a door or hatchway.

1. **IF YOU CAN GET IN,** measure the depth of insulation. If you have 6 inches or more of insulation everywhere, you have enough and you can skip the rest of this page.

2. **IF YOU CAN'T GET INTO THE UNFINISHED PARTS OF YOUR ATTIC AT ALL,** have a contractor measure the insulation for you. Ask him how much is there, and use these figures to complete page 17 and fill out the Energy Checklist.

When you go to take a look at these places, make a note of the depth of insulation that's already there; you'll want this information in a minute.

1. Which method?

You may have already found out that you can't do-it-yourself because you can't get into the unfinished part of your attic. If you can get in, there are some good things you can do yourself to insulate it.

Depending on your particular attic you may be able to do one or more of these:

A. INSULATE ATTIC CEILING

You can insulate your attic ceiling if there's a door to the space above the finished area. You should consider insulating it if there's less than 6 inches already there.

B. INSULATE OUTER ATTIC RAFTERS

"Outer attic rafters" are the parts of the roof shown in the picture below:

You should consider insulating them if:

— there's no insulation between the rafters; and

— there's room for more insulation in the outer attic floor and in the "knee walls" that separate the finished and unfinished parts of the attic.

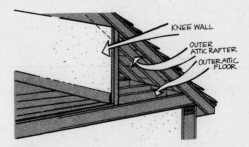

C. INSULATE OUTER ATTIC GABLES

"Outer attic gables" are the little triangular walls shown in the picture. You should insulate them if you insulate the outer attic rafters.

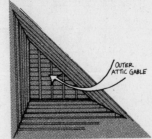

To get a better idea of what's involved in doing-it-yourself, read page 51. See page 42 to see how thick the insulation should be.

If you want to find costs and savings for a do-it-yourself insulation job, use the next page.

If you want to estimate costs and savings for contractor installation, go on to page 18.

Costs and savings for do-it-yourself insulation

1. How big are the areas you want to insulate?

Multiply the length times the width (in feet) of each area that you can insulate.

a. ATTIC CEILING

length X width = area

_____ X _____ = _____

b. OUTER ATTIC RAFTERS (there may be several areas you'll need to add together here)

length X width = area

_____ X _____ = _____

_____ X _____ = _____ add these together

_____ X _____ = _____ total outer attic

+

[_____] rafter area

C. OUTER ATTIC GABLES (the area of these triangles is only half the length times the height.)

length X height ÷2 = area

_____ X _____ ÷2 = _____

Multiply by the number of gable ends to get the total area.

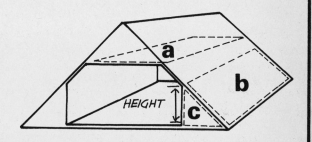

2. Your Savings Factor

For each part of your attic that you've measured, check below about how much insulation is already there. For each row you've checked, multiply your area times the number written to the right:

ATTIC CEILING

☐ none _____ X .38 = _____

☐ 0-2 inches _____ X .09 = _____

☐ 2-4 inches _____ X .04 = _____
                    area

OUTER ATTIC RAFTERS (existing insulation will be in the floor and knee walls)

☐ none _____ X .23 = _____

☐ 0-2 inches _____ X .09 = _____

☐ 2-4 inches _____ X .05 = _____
                    area

OUTER ATTIC GABLES (existing insulation will be in the floor and knee walls)

☐ none _____ X .16 = _____

☐ 0-2 inches _____ X .06 = _____

☐ 2-4 inches _____ X .03 = _____
                    area

+

TOTAL [_____]

Add the results from each row you've filled out to get your Savings Factor.

3. Your Cost

ATTIC CEILING:

If there's no existing insulation:

_____ X $0.18 = _____
area

If there's up to 4 inches of existing insulation:

_____ X $0.09 = _____
area

OUTER ATTIC RAFTERS:

If there's up to 2 inches of existing insulation:

_____ X $0.15 = _____
area

If there's from 2 to 4 inches of existing insulation:

_____ X $0.09 = _____
area

OUTER ATTIC GABLES:

_____ X $0.09 = _____
area

GO TO THE ENERGY CHECKLIST

at the end of the book. On line 3, "Insulate Your Attic," write your total cost in the cost box and your savings factor in the savings box.

Costs and savings for contractor installation

Finished attics differ a lot in how much they cost for a contractor to insulate them. Therefore, this page gives you only a rough estimate of how much it would cost you. If you want a better figure, get a contractor to give you an estimate. To see what's involved, see page 51. To see how much insulation should be installed, see page 42.

Your cost and savings

To get a quick estimate of your cost and savings, follow steps 1, 2, and 3 on this page.

1. How much insulation do you have already?

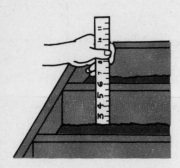

Go up and measure the depth of existing insulation, if you haven't already.

Check the box below that's closest to the depth you find. Usually, there's the same thickness in all parts of the attic. If there are different thicknesses, figure the average depth and check it below:

2. How big is your attic?

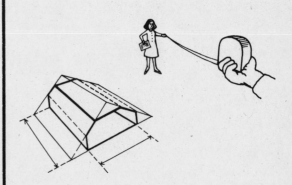

Measure the length and width of the *finished part* of your attic. Round them off to the nearest foot and multiply them together:

length X width = area

_____ X _____ = _____

Check the number of square feet below that's closest to your finished attic area.

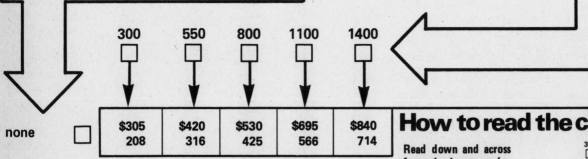

		300	550	800	1100	1400
none	☐	$305 208	$420 316	$530 425	$695 566	$840 714
under 2″	☐	$280 68	$370 97	$450 126	$590 167	$700 205
2″–4″	☐	$220 31	$300 44	$375 56	$490 74	$585 90

How to read the chart

Read down and across from the boxes you've checked to find which square in the chart applies to you, like this:

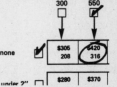

Copy the top number into the cost box on line 3 of the Energy Checklist, "Insulate Your Attic," at the end of the book. Copy the bottom number into the savings box on the same line.

INSULATE YOUR WALLS

Should you insulate them?

It depends on two things: the size of your energy bills and what your walls are like. To find out if you should insulate them, answer these two questions:

1. How big are your energy bills?

If you have just heating — NO whole-house air conditioning, look up the Heating Factor for your city on page 28 or 29. Look at the Heating Factor for the type of heating you have — gas, oil, electricity, or coal. It's one of the numbers in the first four columns.

If your Heating Factor is **0.30** or more, keep on going. If it's less than **0.30,** skip these two pages.

If you have heating AND whole-house air conditioning, look up both your Heating Factor and your Cooling Factor. They're listed on page 28 or 29. Look up the Heating Factor for your city for the type of heating you have — gas, oil, electricity, or coal. It's one of the numbers in the first four columns.

Then look up your Cooling Factor. It's the number in the fifth column.

Add together your Heating and Cooling Factors. If the sum is **0.30** or more, keep going. If it's less than **0.30,** skip these two pages.

2. What are your walls like?

Most houses have *frame* walls. They have a wood structure — usually 2 by 4's — even though they may have brick or stone on the outside.

Some houses have brick or block *masonry* walls that form the structure of the house, without a wooden backup.

If you have frame walls, you should consider insulating them if there's no insulation at all in them already. A contractor can fill them with insulation and cut energy waste through them by 2/3.

You may already know whether or not your walls have insulation in them. If you don't know, here's how to find out: Take the cover off a light switch on an outside wall. *(Turn off the power first.)* Shine a flashlight into the space between the switchbox and the wall material and see if you can see any insulation.

If there's *no* insulation there now, you may need more, so fill out these two pages.

If there *is* some there already, you don't need more, so skip the rest of these pages.

If you have masonry walls, it may be worthwhile to insulate them if they're uninsulated now, even though it's more complicated than insulating frame walls; call a contractor to find out what's involved.

Condensation in Walls

None of the insulating materials contractors blow into frame walls serves as a barrier to moisture vapor; condensation in insulated walls may be a problem:

Look at the map on page 52. If you live in Zone I, and plan to insulate your walls, you need to take steps to ensure that too much moisture from the air in your house won't get into your walls. (In Zone II the problem is much smaller.) If it does, it is likely to condense there in the winter, and you will run two risks: first, that your insulation will become wet and won't insulate; and second, that enough moisture will collect to cause rot in the structure. Here's how to help avoid these dangers:

1. Seal any opening in the inside walls that could afford a path to moisture, especially around the window and door frames.

2. Paint interior walls with a low-permeability paint; this can be a high-gloss enamel or other finish — ask your paint dealer.

TURN TO THE NEXT PAGE FOR YOUR COST AND SAVINGS FACTORS

COSTS AND SAVINGS FOR WALL INSULATION

1. What kind of insulation?

Some kinds of wall insulation cost more than others, and some kinds work better than others. Generally, you get what you pay for — if you spend more, you get better insulation.

The least expensive is *mineral fiber* insulation. There are two kinds; rock wool and glass fiber. Either kind can be blown into the wall by means of a special machine.

A slightly more expensive but more effective insulation is *cellulosic fiber*. This is another loose insulation that's blown in like mineral fiber.

The most expensive and perhaps the most effective insulation is *ureaformaldehyde foam* (*not* urethane foam — urethane foam is not good in walls). Quality control problems with *ureaformaldehyde* foam require that you choose a qualified installer.

2. How big is your house?

Measure the *perimeter* — the total distance around the outside — of each story of your house that has frame walls.

Measure around the heated parts only. Measure in feet to the nearest ten feet.

Write the perimeters for each story over here: ➤

If you have a finished, heated attic, measure the widths of the end walls of the attic *only*. Add up the width of all these walls and write the total to the right: ➤

Add up all the numbers you've written and write the total number of feet of walls here:

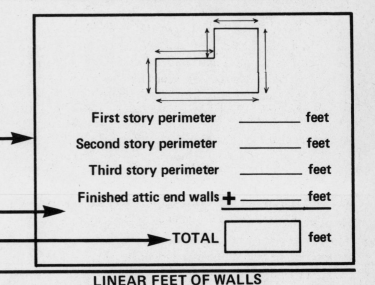

First story perimeter	_____ feet
Second story perimeter	_____ feet
Third story perimeter	_____ feet
Finished attic end walls +	_____ feet
➤ TOTAL [   ] feet

LINEAR FEET OF WALLS

Check the number of feet at the right that's closest to the number of feet of the walls you found above.

		100 LF.	150 LF.	200 LF.	250 LF.	300 LF.	400 LF.
Mineral Fiber	Cost	$320	$480	$640	$800	$960	$1280
	Savings Factor	100	155	205	255	310	410
Cellulosic Fiber	Cost	$360	$540	$720	$900	$1080	$1440
	Savings Factor	110	170	225	280	335	450
Ureaformaldehyde Foam	Cost	$480	$720	$960	$1200	$1440	$1920
	Savings Factor	115	175	230	290	350	460

How to read the chart

The chart shows the cost and savings factors for different kinds of insulation applied to different sizes of houses.

To use the chart, look at the column under the box you've checked.

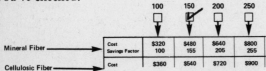

Look at the top numbers in that column—the estimated costs for installing each type of material. See which you can afford; remember that if the cost is higher, your savings will also be higher.

When you've figured out which cost you're willing to pay, copy that cost into the cost box on line 5 of the Energy Checklist at the end of the book, and the savings factor into the savings box on the same line.

INSULATING YOUR CRAWL SPACE WALLS, FLOOR, OR BASEMENT WALLS

If you live in a climate where your heating bill is big enough to be a worry, it's a good idea to insulate the underside of your house. It won't save much on air conditioning, but it will save on heating.

The underside of your house looks like one of these. Choose which of these pictures and descriptions looks like your house, and go to the page indicated.

A. A flat concrete slab sitting on the ground:

There's not much that you can easily do to insulate this type of foundation, and since it's hard to tell how much insulation is already there, it's hard to tell what your savings would be. Therefore, no cost and savings figures are given here for slab insulation. Go on to the next section on page 25.

B. A crawl space with walls around it:

If you have a crawl space that you can seal tightly in winter, you can insulate its walls and the ground around its outer edges. See page 22.

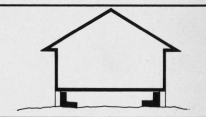

C. A floor over a garage, porch or open crawl space:

If there's an open space under your floor that you can't seal off tightly from the outside air, the place to insulate is in the floor, between the joists. See page 23.

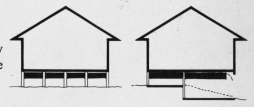

D. Walls of a heated basement that stick out of the ground:

If you have a basement that is heated and used as a living area, it may be worth your while to insulate the basement walls down to a depth of two feet below the ground. See page 24.

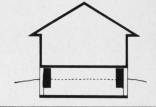

E. A combination of the above types:

Your house may be part heated basement and part crawl space, or some other combination. To estimate your costs and savings, treat each of the parts separately and go to the pages dealing with each part. There are three separate lines on the Energy Checklist:

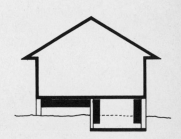

insulate crawl space walls

insulate floor

insulate basement walls

You can fill out as many of these as apply to you, and see which are most important for you to do.

INSULATE YOUR CRAWL SPACE WALLS

If your house (or part of it) sits on top of a crawl space that can be tightly sealed off from the outside air in the winter the cheapest and best place to insulate it is around the outside walls and on the adjacent ground inside the space:

Should you insulate it?

Answer these two questions:

1. Is there *no* insulation at all around the crawl space walls or under the floor?

2. Is your crawl space high enough to get in there to do the work?

If the answer to either of these questions is "No" don't insulate here. Skip the rest of this page. If your answer to both questions is YES, fill out this page.

Your cost and savings

To get a quick estimate of your cost and savings, follow steps 1, 2, and 3 on this page.

1. Measure your crawl space

Measure the distance around the outside of the heated part of your crawl space (don't include areas underneath porches, and other unheated areas).

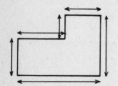

Write that distance down here, in feet (you'll need it in a minute):

_____ feet

2. How much will it cost?

It makes a difference whether you want to do the work yourself or call a contractor. Doing it yourself is hard work, but you'll save a lot of money once you're through. If you're not sure which route you want to take — do-it-yourself or contractor — turn to page 54 to see what doing-it-yourself involves.

TO ESTIMATE THE COST IF YOU'RE DOING-IT-YOURSELF:

Multiply the total distance around your crawl space (the number you wrote in at the bottom of the last column) times $0.40, the cost per running foot:

```
_____ FEET (fill in)
X $ 0.40    PER RUNNING FOOT
$ _____    DO-IT-YOURSELF COST
```

TO ESTIMATE THE COST IF A CONTRACTOR'S DOING THE WORK:

Multiply the distance around your crawl space that you wrote in at the bottom of the last column by $0.70, the cost per running foot.

```
_____ FEET (fill in)
X $ 0.70    PER RUNNING FOOT
$ _____    CONTRACTOR COST
```

3. How much will you save?

To get your savings factor, multiply the distance around your crawl space times .54.

```
_____ FEET (fill in)
X   0.54    RUNNING FOOT SAVINGS
_____    SAVINGS FACTOR
```

Turn to the Energy Checklist at the end of the book. Go to line 4a, called "Insulate Crawl Space Walls". Write your cost in the cost box on that line, and write your savings factor in the savings box on that same line.

INSULATE YOUR FLOOR

There are two cases where it's good to insulate your floor:

1. You have a crawl space that you can't seal off in winter — for example, your house stands on piers:

2. You have a garage, porch, or other cold unheated space with heated rooms above it:

Should you insulate it?

1. Is your floor uninsulated?

2. Is the floor accessible?

   — If it's above a crawl space, is the crawl space high enough for a person to work in it?

No

If your answer to any of these questions is "No" don't insulate the floor. Skip the rest of this page.

Yes

If your answer to both questions is "YES", fill out this page.

Your cost and savings

To get a quick estimate of your cost and savings, follow steps 1, 2, and 3 on this page.

1. Which method?

Decide whether you want to do it yourself or call a contractor. Look at page 56 to help you decide.

2. How big is your floor?

Measure the area of the floor that you plan to insulate.

If It's a Rectangle:
Measure the length and width of the floor in feet and multiply them together.

length	X	width	= area
_____	X	_____	= _____

If It's a Combination of Rectangles:
Break it down into rectangles. For each rectangle, measure its length and its width and multiply them together. Add these numbers to get the total area.

	length	X	width	=	area
1	_____	X	_____	=	_____
2	_____	X	_____	=	_____
3	_____	X	_____	=	_____

total area [ ]

3. How to read the chart

Check the number of square feet below that's closest to the floor area to be insulated that you found above.

Choose either the "do-it-yourself" or "contractor" column in the chart (see 1 above). Read down that column until you come to the row next to the number of square feet you've checked. Circle that box.

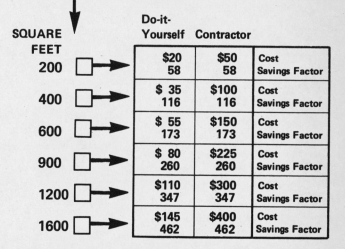

SQUARE FEET	Do-it-Yourself	Contractor	
200	$20 / 58	$50 / 58	Cost / Savings Factor
400	$ 35 / 116	$100 / 116	Cost / Savings Factor
600	$ 55 / 173	$150 / 173	Cost / Savings Factor
900	$ 80 / 260	$225 / 260	Cost / Savings Factor
1200	$110 / 347	$300 / 347	Cost / Savings Factor
1600	$145 / 462	$400 / 462	Cost / Savings Factor

Turn to the Energy Checklist at the end of the book. Go to line 4b, called "Insulate Floor." Write the top number from the box you've circled into the cost box on that line, and the bottom number into the savings box.

INSULATE YOUR BASEMENT WALLS

If you have a basement that you use as a living or work space and that has air outlets, radiators, or baseboard units to heat it, you may find that it will pay to add a layer of insulation to the inside of the wall. You only need to insulate the parts of the walls that are above the ground down to about two feet below the ground, as in the drawing above. Also, the cost figures given below allow for the cost of refinishing as well as insulating.

Should you insulate them?

Are your basement walls insulated? If they aren't, it pays to insulate them in almost any climate if you do the work yourself.

If you can't do it yourself and have to call a contractor, it will probably only pay to insulate these walls if your heating factor is bigger than 0.25.

Your cost and savings

To get a quick estimate of your cost and savings, follow steps 1 and 2 on this page.

1. Make some measurements

Measure the length of each wall that sticks 2 or more feet above ground and add the lengths together.

Write the total number of feet here:_____ feet.
                                  length of wall

Estimate to the nearest foot how far on the average these walls stick up above ground. For example, suppose your house is on a slope like this:

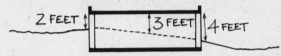

The average height above ground for this house is three feet. Write your average height above ground here:_____ feet.

2. How to use the chart

At the top of the chart, check the height of your basement walls above ground that's closest to the amount you wrote above in Step 1.

At the side of the chart, check either "do-it-yourself" or "contractor".

Read across the row you checked until you come to the column you checked. Circle the square where the row and the column meet.

AVERAGE HEIGHT ABOVE THE GROUND

		2 feet	4 feet	6 feet	8 feet	
		☐	☐	☐	☐	
Do-it-yourself	☐	$2.10	$2.20	$2.35	$2.35	Cost
		.77	1.3	1.9	2.4	Savings Factor
Contractor	☐	$4.60	$5.45	$6.20	$6.20	Cost
		.77	1.3	1.9	2.4	Savings Factor

Multiply the top number in the square you circled times the total length of the walls that you wrote down in Step 1. The result is your estimated total cost.

$_____ X _____ = $_____
top number **length of wall**   **Cost**

Multiply the bottom number in the square that you circled times the total length of the walls to get your savings factor.

_____ X _____ = _____
bottom number **length of wall** **savings factor**

Turn to the Energy Checklist at the end of the book. Go to Line 4c, called "Insulate Basement Walls." Copy the total cost you've found into the cost box on that line and the savings factor into the savings box on the same line.

THERMOSTAT, FURNACE AND AIR CONDITIONER

If you have whole-house air conditioning, you can save about 3 per cent of your air conditioning bill for each degree you turn up your thermostat. Usually, about a 4 degree turn-up will still be comfortable; above that the air conditioning system will have trouble keeping the house cool during the hot part of the day. Figure out how many degrees you can turn up your thermostat, then multiply the number of degrees by 3 to get your percent savings:

$$\underline{\hspace{3cm}} \text{ X 3 = } \underline{\hspace{3cm}}$$
$$\textbf{degree turn-up} \qquad\qquad \textbf{\%savings}$$

YOUR HEATING BILL

The method for figuring out your heating bill depends on what kind of fuel you use. Pick the method below that applies to you:

NOTE: You may heat with two fuels; for example, most of your house may be heated with oil or gas, while some newer rooms may have electric heat. In this case, do this section once for each fuel, and add the results together.

A. Oil or coal heat

If you have an oil or coal furnace that heats your house but *not* your hot water, then all of your oil or coal bill goes to heating. Simply add up your fuel bills for last year. Write the total here:

$$\$ \underline{\hspace{3cm}}$$

If your furnace heats your hot water too, add up your fuel bills for last year and multiply the total by .8:

$$\$\underline{\hspace{2cm}} \text{ X .8 } \$\underline{\hspace{2cm}}$$
$$\textbf{total fuel bill} \qquad \textbf{your heating bill}$$

B. Gas or electric heat

If you have gas heat

OR

If you have electric heat WITHOUT whole-house electric air conditioning:

1. Write your *January* electric or gas bill (whichever kind of heat you have) on line 1 at the top of the next page.

2. Find the city nearest you from the table on page 27 . There's a month written beside the name of that city. Write your electric or gas bill for that month on line 2.

3. Subtract line 2 from line 1 and write the difference on line 3.

4. Write the number from column A of the table for the city nearest you on line 4.

YOUR THERMOSTAT

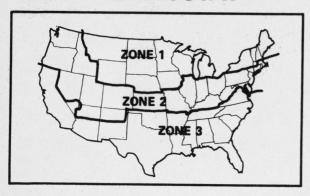

The table below tells you what percent of your heating bill you'll save by turning down your thermostat. Look at the map above to see which zone you live in. Read the column in the table for that zone. Circle either the top or bottom number in that column — you'll need it after you figure out your heating bill.

Circle the top number if you want to see what you'll save with a 5-degree turn-down from your usual setting.

Circle the bottom number if you want to see what you'll save with an 8-degree turn-down from your usual setting.

	ZONE 1	ZONE 2	ZONE 3
5° turn-down	14%	17%	25%
8° turn-down	19%	24%	35%

Table 1

5. Multiply line 3 by line 4; write the result on line 5. That number's your estimated heating bill.

If you have electric heat AND whole-house air conditioning:

Follow steps 1-5 above, except for one thing: in step 4, use the number from column B of the table (instead of column A) for your city, and write it on line 4.

	$ _____	Line 1
SUBTRACT —	$ _____	Line 2
	$ _____	Line 3
MULTIPLY ✗	_____	Line 4
YOUR HEAT BILL	$ _____	Line 5

YOUR AIR CONDITIONING BILL

If you have whole-house air conditioning, estimate how much it's costing you each year — Use this method: Look up the city nearest you in the table on the next page. If there's an asterisk (*) after the name of the city, your air conditioning savings will be insignificant; skip steps 1-5. If there's no asterisk, keep on going.

1. Write your *July* electric bill on line 1 below.

2. Find the city nearest you from the table on the next page. There's a month written beside the name of that city. Write your electric bill for that month on line 2.

3. Subtract line 2 from line 1 and write the difference on line 3.

4. *If you have electric heat* as well as air conditioning, write the number from column D of the table for the city nearest you on line 4. *If you have gas, oil, or coal heat, write* the number from column C of the table for the city nearest you on line 4.

5. Multiply line 3 by line 4: write the result on line 5. That number's your estimated air conditioning bill.

	$ _____	Line 1
SUBTRACT —	$ _____	Line 2
	$ _____	Line 3
MULTIPLY ✗	_____	Line 4
YOUR AIR CONDITIONING BILL	$ _____	Line 5

YOUR DOLLAR SAVINGS

NOW THAT YOU'VE FOUND YOUR HEATING AND AIR CONDITIONING BILLS, YOU'RE READY TO FIND OUT HOW MUCH YOU CAN SAVE EACH YEAR ON THESE MEASURES.

1. YOUR THERMOSTAT

Multiply your heating bill by the percent you circled in table 1 on the previous page and divide by 100:

$$ \$ \underline{\quad\quad} \times \underline{\quad\quad} \div 100 = \underline{\quad\quad} $$
heating bill   % savings   dollar savings

If you have whole-house air conditioning, multiply your air conditioning bill by the percent you figured on the previous page and divide by 100:

$$ \$ \underline{\quad\quad} \times \underline{\quad\quad} \div 100 = \$ \underline{\quad\quad} $$
air cond. bill   % savings   dollar savings

Add up your thermostat savings for heating and air conditioning;

$$ \$ \underline{\quad\quad} + \$ \underline{\quad\quad} = \$ \underline{\quad\quad} $$
heat savings   air cond. savings   total savings

Write your total savings into the second box on line 6 of the Energy Checklist at the end of the book.

2. YOUR OIL OR COAL FURNACE

If you have an oil or coal furnace that hasn't been serviced recently, multiply your heating bill by .1 if you have the furnace serviced.

$$ \$ \underline{\quad\quad} \times 0.1 = \$ \underline{\quad\quad} $$
heating bill   dollar savings

Write the result in the first box on line 7 of the Energy Checklist at the end of the book.*

3. YOUR GAS FURNACE

If you have a gas furnace that hasn't been serviced recently, you can save too — see page 61.

4. YOUR AIR CONDITIONER

If you have a central air conditioner that hasn't been serviced recently, multiply your air conditioning bill by 0.1 if you have the unit serviced.*

$$ \$ \underline{\quad\quad} \times 0.1 = \$ \underline{\quad\quad} $$
air cond. bill   dollar savings

Write the result in the first box on line 8 of the Energy Checklist at the end of the book.

* An estimate of cost has been entered for you on the Energy Checklist. For greater accuracy, use an estimate from your own heating or cooling specialist.

Location	Month	Gas Electric Heat Alone (A)	Electric Heat With Electric A/C (B)	Electric A/C Alone (C)	Electric A/C With Electric Heat (D)
Alabama					
Montgomery	May	4.2	5.2	7.3	7.3
Alaska					
Anchorage	July	7.8	7.8	*	*
Arizona					
Flagstaff	July	6.4	6.6	*	*
Phoenix	April	4.4	5.1	5.1	6.3
Arkansas					
Little Rock	May	4.3	4.7	5.6	5.9
California					
Bishop	Sept.	5.2	7.5	3.5	5.1
Eureka	July	17.0	17.0	*	*
Los Angeles	Oct.	6.0	7.1	10.5	***
Bakersfield	April	4.8	5.3	4.9	8.0
San Francisco	Sept.	6.7	7.0	*	*
Colorado					
Alamosa	July	6.0	6.0	*	*
Denver	Sept.	6.2	6.3	3.5	*
Connecticut					
New Haven	Sept.	5.8	6.1	4.7	**
Delaware					
Dover	May	5.7	5.8	3.8	9.6
District of Columbia					
Washington	May	5.3	5.5	4.3	6.7
Florida					
Miami	Feb.	†	†	9.6	9.6
Tallahassee	April	4.4	4.9	5.6	6.5
Georgia					
Atlanta	May	4.8	5.2	4.7	5.4
Savannah	April	4.6	5.1	5.3	6.5
Idaho					
Boise	Sept.	5.9	6.0	3.1	**
Illinois					
Chicago	Sept.	5.5	5.8	5.2	**
Springfield	May	5.4	5.5	3.6	**
Cairo	May	4.7	4.9	4.2	5.3
Indiana					
Indianapolis	Sept.	5.6	6.1	6.5	**
Iowa					
Des Moines	Sept.	5.1	5.4	11.8	**
Dubuque	Sept.	5.8	6.0	4.1	*
Kansas					
Wichita	May	4.9	5.0	3.5	5.8
Goodland	Sept.	5.7	5.8	3.4	9.8
Kentucky					
Lexington	May	5.6	5.6	4.0	11.4
Louisiana					
Baton Rouge	April	4.1	4.8	5.9	6.5
Skreveport	April	4.6	5.0	4.9	7.7
Maine					
Portland	July	5.7	5.7	*	*
Maryland					
Baltimore	May	5.5	5.6	3.9	9.0
Massachusetts					
Worcester	Sept.	6.2	6.4	4.4	*
Michigan					
Lansing	July	5.5	5.5	*	*
Minnesota					
Duluth	July	6.0	6.1	*	*
Minneapolis	May	6.2	6.3	2.8	*
Mississippi					
Jackson	April	4.9	5.3	5.0	7.7
Missouri					
St. Louis	May	4.8	4.8	3.4	5.9
Springfield	May	5.6	5.7	3.7	9.1
Montana					
Helena	July	5.8	6.0	*	*
Nebraska					
Omaha	Sept.	5.3	5.5	4.3	*
Scottsbluff	Sept.	6.1	6.2	3.1	*

Location	Month	Gas Or Electric Heat Alone (A)	Electric Heat With Electric A/C (B)	Electric A/C Alone (C)	Electric A/C With Electric Heat (D)
Nevada					
Elko	Sept.	6.8	6.8	2.2	*
Las Vegas	April	4.7	4.9	4.1	5.7
New Hampshire					
Concord	July	5.5	5.9	*	*
New Jersey					
Atlantic City	Sept.	5.4	5.7	5.1	8.2
New Mexico					
Raton	Sept.	6.3	6.5	3.7	*
Silver City	Sept.	4.7	5.3	5.7	5.9
New York					
New York City	Sept.	5.1	5.6	5.9	8.0
Rochester	Sept.	6.1	6.4	5.0	*
North Carolina					
Raleigh	May	4.9	5.2	5.3	6.9
Wilmington	May	4.3	4.8	7.0	5.9
North Dakota					
Bismarck	July	5.3	5.5	*	*
Ohio					
Youngstown	Sept.	6.1	4.8	5.2	*
Cincinnati	May	5.4	5.4	4.0	10.0
Oklahoma					
Oklahoma City	May	4.5	4.8	4.9	6.1
Oregon					
Salem	July	6.1	6.5	*	*
Medford	May	7.4	6.3	3.3	11.3
Pennsylvania					
Philadelphia	May	5.7	5.8	3.8	10.5
Pittsburgh	Sept.	5.9	6.2	5.4	*
Rhode Island					
Providence	Sept.	5.9	6.1	4.7	*
South Carolina					
Charleston	April	4.7	4.9	4.9	6.2
Greenville-Spartanburg	May	4.6	5.0	4.8	5.4
South Dakota					
Rapid City	Sept.	6.3	6.3	3.2	*
Tennessee					
Knoxville	May	5.1	5.3	4.7	6.5
Memphis	May	4.3	4.8	5.2	5.6
Texas					
Austin	April	4.1	4.5	5.5	7.0
Dallas	April	4.6	5.0	5.0	7.7
Houston	April	4.0	4.8	5.9	7.0
Lubbock	May	4.7	5.2	6.8	9.3
Utah					
Salt Lake City	Sept.	5.6	5.7	3.2	6.4
Milford	Sept.	5.5	5.7	2.7	*
Vermont					
Burlington	July	5.6	5.9	*	*
Virginia					
Richmond	May	5.1	5.4	5.2	8.0
Washington					
Olympia	July	6.8	7.0	*	*
Walla Walla	Sept.	5.3	5.6	3.3	8.0
West Virginia					
Charleston	May	5.7	5.7	4.2	9.6
Elkins	Sept.	6.5	5.2	4.0	*
Wisconsin					
Milwaukee	July	5.7	6.2	*	*
Wyoming					
Casper	Sept.	6.7	6.8	2.8	*

*Air conditioning savings not significant.

**Your air conditioning bill is about 1/10 of your electric heating bill.

***Your air conditioning bill is about 1/4 of your electric heating bill.

†Heating savings not significant.

YOUR HEATING AND COOLING FACTORS

You already have all the Savings Factors for the energy-saving home improvements you're considering. Combine them with your Heating Factor and (if you have whole-house air conditioning) your Cooling Factor, and you'll get dollar savings. There's *one* Heating Factor, and *one* Cooling Factor for your house, and they are based on where you live, and how much you pay for the fuel you use for heating (and cooling). The Table on this page and the next has your Heating and Cooling Factors in it. There are two ways to use the Table: a quick approximate way, and a slower but more accurate way that uses your own fuel bill to get your own Factors.

1. The quick way

Find the row on the chart below that's for the city nearest you. Look at the first four columns in that row (A,B,C,D). Circle the number for your fuel. It's your Heating Factor.

If you have whole-house air conditioning, also circle the number in column E of the same row. That's your **Cooling Factor**

Important: Check the fuel prices given in columns F through I. They were collected in mid-1974 and were used to figure the Heating and Cooling Factors given in Columns A through E. Compare them with the price you pay for fuel (see "How Much Do You Really Pay for Fuel" below). If you find a significant difference, figure your Heating and Cooling Factors in " 2. Using Your Own Bill" below.

Instructions for using these Factors are on the Energy Checklist at the end of the book.

2. Using your own bill

You can calculate your Heating Factor (and your Cooling Factor, if you have whole-house air conditioning), using the figures from your own utility bills.

To figure your exact Heating Factor, find the Heating Multiplier for your city and your fuel (Columns J-M), and multiply it by the price you pay for heating fuel. Make sure you use the right units: gas– ¢/100 Cu.Ft., oil – ¢/gal., electricity – ¢/Kwh, coal – ¢/lb. (see "How Much Do You Really Pay for Fuel"):

_____ X _____ = _____
your fuel price   your Heating   Heating Factor
                    Multiplier   Enter on the
                                          Energy Checklist

To figure out your exact Cooling Factor, find the Cooling Multiplier in Column N for your city, and multiply it by the price you pay for electricity in **cents** per kilowatt hour, (see "How Much Do You Really Pay for Fuel"):

_____ X _____ = _____
electricity price   your Cooling   Cooling Factor
(¢/Kwh)   Multiplier   Enter on the
                                         Energy Checklist

How Much Do You Really Pay for Fuel?

Your true cost for 100 cu. ft. of gas, a kilowatt of electricity, etc., is sometimes pretty well hidden in your bill. Call your utility company and ask them for the true cost (including all "fuel adjustment" factors and taxes) of the *last* unit of fuel that you buy every month. Use this cost to figure your Heating and Cooling Factor.

		Heating Factors				Cooling Factor	Fuel costs				Heating Multipliers				Cooling Multiplier
		Gas	Oil	Elec	Coal		Gas ¢/100 cu. ft.	Oil ¢/gal.	Elec ¢/Kwh	Coal ¢/lb.	Gas	Oil	Elec	Coal	
		A	B	C	D	E	F	G	H	I	J	K	L	M	N
ALABAMA	Montgomery	.16	*	.61	.29	.23	15.00	*	2.71	2.95	.0105	*	.2260	.0987	.0859
ALASKA	Anchorage	.33	*	1.53	*	.00	12.00	*	2.57	*	.0275	*	.5956		.0001
ARIZONA	Flagstaff	.29	*	1.48	*	.02	12.50	*	2.93	*	.0233	*	.5040	*	.0056
	Phoenix	.10	*	.44	*	.36	12.50	*	2.50	*	.0081	*	.1741	*	.1430
ARKANSAS	Little Rock	.15	*	1.05	*	.25	10.00	*	3.30	*	.0147	*	.3176	*	.0769
CALIFORNIA	Bishop	.16	*	.85	*	.10	9.80	*	2.41	*	.0163	*	.3515	*	.0414
	Eureka	.21	*	1.23	*	.00	9.80	*	2.69	*	.0212	*	.4580	*	.0001
	Los Angeles	.07	*	.42	*	.09	9.50	*	2.50	*	.0078	*	.1682	*	.0367
	Bakersfield	.08	*	.51	*	.23	8.00	*	2.46	*	.0097	*	.2093	*	.0941
	San Francisco	.14	*	.71	*	.01	10.00	*	2.40	*	.0137	*	.2967	*	.0059
COLORADO	Alamosa	.24	*	1.44	*	.01	8.80	*	2.39	*	.0278	*	.6010	*	.0023
	Denver	.10	*	.84	*	.05	6.00	*	2.30	*	.0168	*	.3640		.0231

| State | City | Heating Factors | | | | Cooling Factor | Fuel costs | | | | Heating Multipliers | | | | Cooling Multiplier |
| | | Gas | Oil | Elec | Coal | | Gas ¢/100 cu. ft. | Oil ¢/gal. | Elec ¢/Kwh | Coal ¢/lb. | Gas | Oil | Elec | Coal | |
		A	B	C	D	E	F	G	H	I	J	K	L	M	N
CONNECTICUT	New Haven	.33	.51	1.37	*	.10	17.10	35.35	3.29	*	.0192	.0143	.4155	*	.0312
DELAWARE	Dover	.29	.47	1.35	.56	.15	15.30	33.37	3.32	3.18	.0188	.0140	.4054	.1770	.0447
D. C.	Washington	.21	.44	1.15	.54	.18	13.00	36.36	3.30	3.54	.0161	.0120	.3473	.1517	.0559
FLORIDA	Miami	.02	.03	.06	*	.48	25.00	35.90	3.00	*	.0010	.0007	.0211	*	.1589
	Tallahasee	.08	.18	.42	*	.27	11.70	35.90	2.87	*	.0068	.0051	.1465	*	.0941
GEORGIA	Atlanta	.14	*	.61	.43	.15	12.50	*	2.50	4.04	.0113	*	.2435	.1063	.0612
	Savannah	.10	*	.48	*	.24	12.50	*	2.68	*	.0083	*	.1794	*	.0892
IDAHO	Boise	.21	.48	.78	*	.07	12.80	38.90	2.17	*	.0166	.0124	.3582	*	.0330
ILLINOIS	Chicago	.19	.47	1.38	.71	.13	10.20	34.50	3.50	4.15	.0182	.0136	.3944	.1722	.0373
	Springfield	.10	.35	.63	.54	.10	7.40	34.50	2.11	4.15	.0138	.0103	.2976	.1300	.0453
	Cairo	.12	.32	.70	.40	.17	10.00	34.50	2.60	3.42	.0125	.0093	.2692	.1176	.0663
INDIANA	Indianapolis	.15	.40	.77	.59	.09	9.00	33.20	2.20	3.82	.0163	.0121	.3514	.1534	.0398
IOWA	Des Moines	.15	.48	1.16	*	.12	8.20	34.18	2.85	*	.0188	.0140	.4062	*	.0406
	Dubuque	.21	.54	1.42	*	.08	9.90	34.18	3.12	*	.0210	.0157	.4548	*	.0257
KANSAS	Wichita	.09	*	.63	*	.12	6.20	*	1.92	*	.0151	*	.3255	*	.0603
	Goodland	.09	*	.82	*	.07	5.30	*	2.17	*	.0175	*	.3786	*	.0337
KENTUCKY	Lexington	.17	.34	.79	.35	.10	11.20	30.25	2.39	2.42	.0153	.0114	.3300	.1441	.0423
LOUISIANA	Baton Rouge	.05	*	.42	*	.29	7.10	*	2.76	*	.0071	*	.1539	*	.1046
	Shreveport	.23	*	.50	*	.21	23.50	*	2.30	*	.0100	*	.2155	*	.0914
MAINE	Portland	*	.61	1.40	*	.04	*	38.10	3.02	*	*	.0161	.4631	*	.0138
MARYLAND	Baltimore	.28	.45	1.30	.49	.17	16.50	36.36	3.60	3.12	.0167	.0124	.3603	.1573	.0461
MASSACHUSETTS	Worcester	.55	.61	1.63	*	.06	24.10	35.90	3.32	*	.0227	.0169	.4911	*	.0185
MICHIGAN	Lansing	.23	.51	.91	.57	.04	11.50	34.85	2.14	3.04	.0197	.0147	.4260	.1860	.0200
MINNESOTA	Duluth	.45	*	1.86	*	.02	17.80	*	3.39	*	.0254	*	.5482	*	.0073
	Minneapolis	.22	*	1.27	*	.07	10.50	*	2.76	*	.0213	*	.4595	*	.0268
MISSISSIPPI	Jackson	.10	*	.57	.29	.24	10.00	*	2.60	3.00	.0102	*	.2209	.0964	.0918
MISSOURI	St. Louis	.15	*	.66	*	.11	9.80	*	2.00	*	.0153	*	.3306	*	.0540
	Springfield	.16	*	.76	*	.11	9.80	*	2.19	*	.0160	*	.3453	*	.0518
MONTANA	Helena	.18	*	1.23	*	.03	8.81	*	2.76	*	.0206	*	.4456	*	.0093
NEBRASKA	Omaha	.18	.48	.86	*	.09	9.40	33.79	2.12	*	.0189	.0141	.4077	*	.0446
	Scottsbluff	.14	.43	.72	*	.05	8.00	33.79	1.98	*	.0169	.0126	.3658	*	.0232
NEVADA	Elko	.28	.51	1.13	*	.04	14.90	36.10	2.77	*	.0188	.0141	.4075	*	.0128
	Las Vegas	.12	.28	.39	*	.19	11.30	36.10	1.73	*	.0103	.0077	.2228	*	.1114
NEW HAMPSHIRE	Concord	.37	.56	1.26	*	.05	17.40	35.54	2.76	*	.0211	.0157	.4552	*	.0170
NEW JERSEY	Atlanta City	.20	.48	1.30	.58	.10	11.00	35.30	3.28	3.33	.0183	.0137	.3957	.1728	.0312
NEW MEXICO	Raton	.15	*	1.01	*	.09	7.50	*	2.30	*	.0203	*	.4388	*	.0391
	Silver City	.06	*	.68	*	.10	5.00	*	2.61	*	.0121	*	.2611	*	.0391
NEW YORK	New York City	.33	.49	3.05	.68	.33	18.00	35.59	7.70	3.95	.0183	.0137	.3959	.1729	.0434
	Rochester	.35	.58	.95	.45	.05	16.10	35.59	2.00	2.16	.0220	.0164	.4755	.2076	.0259
NORTH CAROLINA	Raleigh	.27	.41	.77	.57	.12	17.30	35.29	2.30	3.90	.0155	.0115	.3347	.1462	.0500
	Wilmington	.14	.28	.57	.42	.18	13.00	35.29	2.47	4.15	.0107	.0080	.2315	.1011	.0730
NORTH DAKOTA	Bismarck	.20	*	1.36	*	.05	8.80	*	2.80	*	.0224	*	.4852	*	.0171
OHIO	Youngstown	.27	.55	1.57	.72	.07	12.70	35.20	3.47	3.64	.0209	.0156	.4522	.1974	.0204
	Cincinnati	.18	.38	.75	.49	.11	12.30	35.20	2.40	3.61	.0144	.0107	.3107	.1357	.0439
OKLAHOMA	Oklahoma City	.12	*	.60	*	.16	9.50	*	2.30	*	.0121	*	.2625	*	.0705
OREGON	Salem	.62	.59	.59	*	.01	28.50	36.20	1.26	*	.0217	.0162	.4690	*	.0101
	Medford	.39	.62	.90	*	.05	17.00	36.20	1.83	*	.0229	.0170	.4940	*	.0283
PENNSYLVANIA	Philadelphia	.35	.49	1.31	.52	.15	18.90	35.90	3.30	3.03	.0183	.0137	.3959	.1729	.0448
	Pittsburgh	.18	.48	1.06	.32	.03	9.90	35.90	2.72	1.90	.0180	.0134	.3890	.1698	.0120
RHODE ISLAND	Providence	.42	.49	1.47	*	.10	21.50	33.68	3.50	*	.0194	.0145	.4195	*	.0285
SOUTH CAROLINA	Charleston	.15	.19	.49	*	.23	17.00	29.50	2.61	*	.0087	.0065	.1888	*	.0869
	Greenville-Spartanburg	.16	.25	.51	*	.12	14.00	29.50	2.08	*	.0113	.0085	.2450	*	.0561
SOUTH DAKOTA	Rapid City	.16	.50	1.10	*	.06	8.80	36.15	2.74	*	.0186	.0139	.4027	*	.0209
TENNESSEE	Knoxville	.19	.30	.43	.32	.08	14.00	30.23	1.50	2.59	.0133	.0099	.2873	.1255	.0557
	Memphis	.13	.27	.41	.29	.12	10.90	30.23	1.58	2.59	.0119	.0089	.2569	.1122	.0780
TEXAS	Austin	.07	*	.32	*	.21	8.60	*	1.92	*	.0078	*	.1688	*	.1071
	Dallas	.09	*	.42	*	.23	9.70	*	2.17	*	.0090	*	.1943	*	.1049
	Houston	.08	*	.25	*	.19	13.00	*	1.93	*	.0061	*	.1319	*	.1000
	Lubbock	.09	*	.57	*	.14	7.80	*	2.27	*	.0117	*	.2521	*	.0617
UTAH	Salt Lake City	.15	*	.85	*	.07	7.70	*	2.00	*	.0197	*	.4264	*	.0371
	Milford	.16	*	.98	*	.06	7.70	*	2.13	*	.0212	*	.4578	*	.0267
VERMONT	Burlington	*	.58	1.27	*	.04	*	33.10	2.50	*	*	.0176	.5098	*	.0178
VIRGINIA	Richmond	.25	.40	.86	.57	.14	17.30	36.55	2.70	4.13	.0147	.0110	.3178	.1388	.0537
WASHINGTON	Olympia	.32	.65	.63	*	.00	13.50	36.40	1.21	*	.0239	.0178	.5165	*	.0035
	Walla Walla	.21	.37	.47	*	.06	15.40	36.40	1.59	*	.0137	.0102	.2963	*	.0357
WEST VIRGINIA	Charleston	.12	.43	.69	.21	.09	8.40	39.40	2.20	1.54	.0146	.0109	.3154	.1377	.0388
	Elkins	.16	.54	1.00	.27	.05	8.40	39.40	2.50	1.54	.0185	.0138	.3999	.1746	.0208
WISCONSIN	Milwaukee	.28	.57	1.27	.72	.06	13.00	35.40	2.70	3.48	.0218	.0162	.4707	.2055	.0216
WYOMING	Casper	.11	*	1.00	*	.04	6.00	*	2.47	*	.0188	*	.4062	*	.0151

* **Data not collected**

PART 3: HOW TO DO IT

This part is divided into sections, each one treating an energy-saving step—
13 in all. A section works like this:

First, how hard is it ?

Should you do it yourself? - a quick rundown to help you decide whether
you can handle it yourself or if you need the services of a professional.

Then, how to get it done

If you're doing it yourself:
    Tools you'll need   How much material
    Safety items to include   Getting it done, step by step
    What kind of materials

OR if you want to hire a contractor to do it, how to make sure he does the
job right.
    What kind of materials   Signing a contract
    How much material   What to check
    R-Value

Last, more information you may need

Some general information that could be helpful:
    Buying Insulating Materials
    Choosing a Contractor
    Getting Financing

CAULK THE OPENINGS IN YOUR HOME

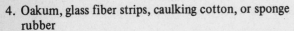

AN EASY DO-IT-YOURSELF PROJECT

Caulking should be applied wherever two different materials or parts of the house meet. It takes no specialized skill to apply and a minimum of tools.

Tools

1. Ladder
2. Caulking gun
3. Caulking cartridges
4. Oakum, glass fiber strips, caulking cotton, or sponge rubber
5. Putty knife or large screwdriver

Safety

You'll need to use a ladder to reach some of the areas which need to be caulked. Be sure you use it safely.

Level and block the ladder in place. Have a helper hold it if possible.

Don't try to reach that extra little bit — get down and move the ladder.

Carry your caulking gun with a sling so that you can use both hands climbing the ladder.

Where a house needs to be caulked

1. Between window drip caps (tops of windows) and siding.
2. Between door drip caps and siding.
3. At joints between window frames and siding.
4. At joints between door frames and siding.
5. Between window sills and siding.
6. At corners formed by siding.
7. At sills where wood structure meets the foundation.
8. Outside water faucets, or other special breaks in the outside house surface.
9. Where pipes and wires penetrate the ceiling below an unheated attic.
10. Between porches and main body of the house.
11. Where chimney or masonry meets siding.
12. Where storm windows meet the window frame, except for drain holes at window sill.
13. And if you have a heated attic; where the wall meets the eave at the gable ends.

Materials

What you'll need

Caulking compound is available in these basic types:

1. Oil or resin base caulk; readily available and will bond to most surfaces — wood, masonry and metal; not very durable but lowest in first cost for this type of application.
2. Latex, butyl or polyvinyl based caulk; all readily available and will bond to most surfaces, more durable, but more expensive than oil or resin based caulk.
3. Elastomeric caulks; most durable and most expensive; includes silicones, polysulfides and polyurethanes; the instructions provided on the labels should be followed.
4. Filler; includes oakum, caulking cotton, sponge rubber, and glass fiber types; used to fill extra wide cracks or as a backup for elastomeric caulks.

CAUTION: Lead base caulk is not recommended because it is toxic. Many states prohibit its use.

How much

Estimating the number of cartridges of caulking compound required is difficult since the number needed will vary greatly with the size of cracks to be filled. Rough estimates are:

1/2 cartridge per window or door

4 cartridges for the foundation sill

2 cartridges for a two story chimney

If possible, it's best to start the job with a half-dozen cartridges and then purchase more as the job continues and you need them.

Installation

1

Before applying caulking compound, clean area of paint build-up, dirt, or deteriorated caulk with solvent and putty knife or large screwdriver.

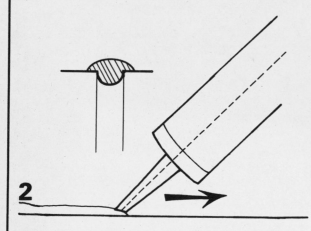

2

Drawing a good bead of caulk will take a little practice. First attempts may be a bit messy. Make sure the bead overlaps both sides for a tight seal.

3

A wide bead may be necessary to make sure caulk adheres to both sides.

4

Fill extra wide cracks like those at the sills (where the house meets the foundation) with oakum, glass fiber insulation strips, etc.)

FOUNDATION SILL

5

In places where you can't quite fill the gaps, finish the job with caulk.

6

Caulking compound also comes in rope form. Unwind it and force it into cracks with your fingers. You can fill extra long cracks easily this way.

WEATHERSTRIP YOUR WINDOWS

AN EASY DO-IT-YOURSELF PROJECT

Weatherstripping windows can be accomplished by even the inexperienced handyman. A minimum of tools and skills is required.

Tools

1. Hammer and nails
2. Screwdriver
3. Tin snips
4. Tape measure

Safety

Upper story windows may be a problem. You should be able to do all work from inside, but avoid awkward leaning out of windows when tacking weatherstripping into place. If you find you need to use a ladder observe the precautions on page 32.

Materials
What you'll need

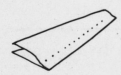

Thin spring metal

Installed in the channel of window so it is virtually invisible. Somewhat difficult to install. Very durable.

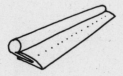

Rolled vinyl

With or without metal backing. Visible when installed. Easy to install. Durable.

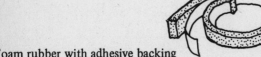

Foam rubber with adhesive backing

Easy to install. Breaks down and wears rather quickly. Not as effective a sealer as metal strips or rolled vinyl.

Never use where friction occurs.

How much

Weatherstripping is purchased either by the running foot or in kit form for each window. In either case you'll have to make a list of your windows, and measure them to find the total length of weatherstripping you'll need. Measure the total distance around the edges of the moving parts of each window type you have, and complete the list below:

Type	Size	Quantity	X length req'd	= Total
1. Double-hung	1	(_____)	X (_____)	= _____
	2	(_____)	X (_____)	= _____
	3	(_____)	X (_____)	= _____
2. Casement	1	(_____)	X (_____)	= _____
	2	(_____)	X (_____)	= _____
	3	(_____)	X (_____)	= _____
3. Tilting	1	(_____)	X (_____)	= _____
	2	(_____)	X (_____)	= _____
	3	(_____)	X (_____)	= _____
4. Sliding pane	1	(_____)	X (_____)	= _____
	2	(_____)	X (_____)	= _____
	3	(_____)	X (_____)	= _____

Total length of weatherstripping required _____

Be sure to allow for waste. If you buy in kit form, be sure the kit is intended for your window type and size.

Installation

Thin spring metal

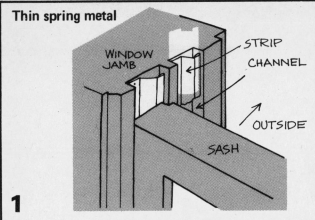

1

Install by moving sash to the open position and sliding strip in between the sash and the channel. Tack in place into the casing. Do not cover the pulleys in the upper channels.

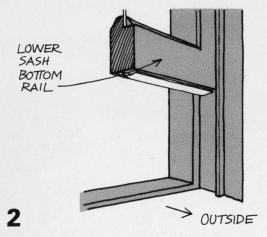

2

Install strips the full width of the sash on the bottom of the lower sash bottom rail and the top of the upper sash top rail.

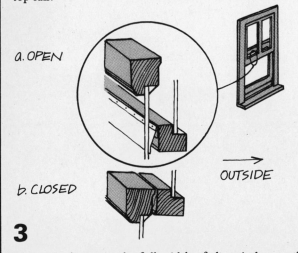

3

Then attach a strip the full width of the window to the upper sash bottom rail. Countersink the nails slightly so they won't catch on the lower sash top rail.

Rolled vinyl

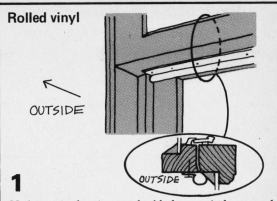

1

Nail on vinyl strips on double-hung windows as shown. A sliding window is much the same and can be treated as a double-hung window turned on its side. Casement and

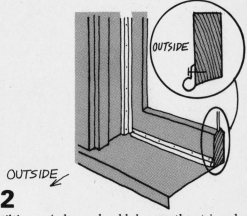

2

tilting windows should be weatherstripped with the vinyl nailed to the window casing so that, as the window shuts, it compresses the roll.

Adhesive-backed foam strip

Install adhesive backed foam, on all types of windows, only where there is no friction. On double-hung windows, this is only on the bottom (as shown) and top rails. Other types of windows can use foam strips in many more places.

WEATHERSTRIP YOUR DOORS

AN EASY DO-IT-YOURSELF PROJECT

You can weatherstrip your doors even if you're not an experienced handyman. There are several types of weatherstripping for doors, each with its own level of effectiveness, durability and degree of installation difficulty. Select among the options given the one you feel is best for you. The installations are the same for the two sides and top of a door, with a different, more durable one for the threshold.

The Alternative Methods and Materials

1. Adhesive backed foam:

Tools

Knife or shears,
Tape measure

TOP VIEW

Evaluation — extremely easy to install, invisible when installed, not very durable, more effective on doors than windows.

Installation — stick foam to inside face of jamb.

2. Rolled vinyl with aluminum channel backing:

Tools

Hammer, nails,
Tin snips
Tape measure

TOP VIEW

Evaluation — easy to install, visible when installed, durable.

Installation — nail strip snugly against door on the casing

3. Foam rubber with wood backing:

Tools

Hammer, nails,
Hand saw,
Tape measure

TOP VIEW

Evaluation — easy to install, visible when installed, not very durable.

Installation — nail strip snugly against the closed door. Space nails 8 to 12 inches apart.

4. Spring metal:

Tools

Tin snips
Hammer, nails,
Tape measure

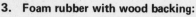

TOP VIEW

Evaluation — easy to install, invisible when installed, extremely durable.

Installation — cut to length and tack in place. Lift outer edge of strip with screwdriver after tacking, for better seal.

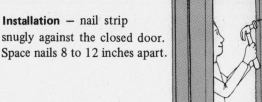

Note: These methods are harder than 1 through 4.

5. Interlocking metal channels:

Tools

Hack saw,
Hammer, nails,
Tape measure

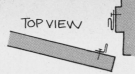

Evaluation — difficult to install (alignment is critical), visible when installed, durable but subject to damage, because they're exposed, excellent seal.

Installation — cut and fit strips to head of door first: male strip on door, female on head; then hinge side of door: male strip on jamb, female on door; finally lock side on door, female on jamb.

6. Fitted interlocking metal channels: (J-Strips)

Evaluation — very difficult to install, exceptionally good weather seal, invisible when installed, not exposed to possible damage.

Installation — should be installed by a carpenter. Not appropriate for do-it-yourself installation unless done by an accomplished handyman.

7. Sweeps:

Tools

Screwdriver,
Hack saw,
Tape measure

Evaluation — useful for flat threshholds, may drag on carpet or rug.

Installation — cut sweep to fit 1/16 inch in from the edges of the door. Some sweeps are installed on the inside and some outside. Check instructions for your particular type.

8. Door Shoes:

Tools

Screwdriver,
Hack saw,
Plane,
Tape measure

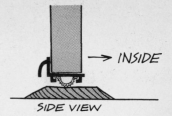

Evaluation — useful with wooden threshhold that is not worn, very durable, difficult to install (must remove door).

Installation — remove door and trim required amount off bottom. Cut to door width. Install by sliding vinyl out and fasten with screws.

9. Vinyl bulb threshold:

Tools

Screwdriver,
Hack saw,
Plane,
Tape measure

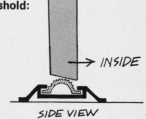

Evaluation — useful where there is no threshhold or wooden one is worn out, difficult to install, vinyl will wear but replacements are available.

Installation — remove door and trim required amount off bottom. Bottom should have about 1/8" bevel to seal against vinyl. Be sure bevel is cut in right direction for opening.

10. Interlocking threshold:

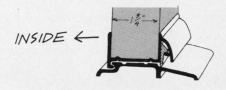

Evaluation — very difficult to install, exceptionally good weather seal.

Installation — should be installed by a skilled carpenter.

INSTALL PLASTIC STORM WINDOWS

AN EASY DO-IT-YOURSELF PROJECT

Tack the plastic sheets over the outside of your windows or tape sheets over the inside instead of installing permanent type storm windows.

Tools & Materials

1. Six-mil thick polyethylene plastic in rolls or kits
2. Shears to cut and trim plastic
3. 2" wide masking tape

   OR

3. Hammer and tacks
4. 1/4" X 1-1/4" wood slats

Installation

Measure the width of your larger windows to determine the width of the plastic rolls to buy. Measure the length of your windows to see how many linear feet and

therefore how many rolls or the kit size you need to buy.

Attach to the inside or outside of the frame so that the plastic will block airflow that leaks around the moveable parts of the window. If you attach the plastic to the outside use the slats and tacks. If you attach it to the inside masking tape will work.

Inside installation is easier and will provide greater protection to the plastic. Outside installation is more difficult, especially on a 2 story house, and the plastic is more likely to be damaged by the elements.

Be sure to install tightly and securely, and remove all excess — besides looking better, this will make the plastic less susceptible to deterioration during the course of the winter.

INSTALL SINGLE PANE STORM WINDOWS

CONTRACTOR ASSEMBLY

DO-IT-YOURSELF INSTALLATION

Storm window suppliers will build single pane storm windows to your measurements that you then install yourself. Another method is to make your own with aluminum do-it-yourself materials available at most hardware stores.

Installation

Determine how you want the windows to sit in the frame. Your measurements will be the outside measurements of the storm window. Be as accurate as possible, then allow 1/8" along each edge for clearance. You'll be responsible for any errors in measurement, so do a good job.

When your windows are delivered, check the actual measurements carefully against your order.

Install the windows and fix in place with moveable clips so you can take them down every summer.

Advantages and Disadvantages

Single pane storm windows aren't as expensive as the double-track or triple-track combination windows (see page 40). The major disadvantage of the single pane windows is that you can't open them easily after they're installed.

Selection: Judging Quality

Frame finish: A mill finish (plain aluminum) will oxidize quickly and degrade appearance. Windows with an anodized or baked enamel finish look better.

Weatherstripping: The side of the aluminum frame which touches the window frame should have a permanently installed weather strip or gasket to seal the crack between the window and the single pane storm window frames.

INSTALL COMBINATION STORM WINDOWS

CONTRACTOR INSTALLED

Triple track, combination (windows and screen) storm windows are designed for installation over double hung windows. They are permanently installed and can be opened any time with a screen slid into place for ventilation.

Double-track combination units are also available and they cost less. Both kinds are sold almost everywhere, and can be bought with or without the cost of installation.

Installation

You can save a few dollars (10% to 15% of the purchase price) by installing the windows yourself. But you'll need some tools: caulking gun, drill, and screw driver. In most cases it will be easier to have the supplier install your windows for you, although it will cost more.

The supplier will first measure all the windows where you want storm windows installed. It will take anywhere from several days to a few weeks to make up your order before the supplier returns to install them.

Installation should take less than one day, depending on how many windows are involved. Two very important items should be checked to make sure the installation is properly done.

Make sure that both the window sashes and screen sash move smoothly and seal tightly when closed after installation. Poor installation can cause misalignment.

Be sure there is a *tightly* caulked seal around the edge of the storm windows. Leaks can hurt the performance of storm windows a lot.

> **NOTE:** Most combination units will come with two or three 1/4" dia. holes (or other types of vents) drilled through the frame where it meets the window sill. This is to keep winter condensation from collecting on the sill and causing rot. Keep these holes clear, and drill them yourself if your combination units don't already have them.

Selection: Judging Quality

Frame finish: A mill finish (plain aluminum) will oxidize, reducing ease of operation and degrading appearance. An anodized or baked enamel finish is better.

Corner joints: Quality of construction affects the strength and performance of storm windows. Corners are a good place to check construction. They should be strong and air tight. Normally overlapped corner joints are better than mitered. If you can see through the joints, they will leak air.

Sash tracks and weatherstripping: Storm windows are supposed to reduce air leakage around windows. The depth of the metal grooves (sash tracks) at the sides of the window and the weatherstripping quality makes a big difference in how well storm windows can do this. Compare several types before deciding.

Hardware quality: The quality of locks and catches has a direct effect on durability and is a good indicator of overall construction quality.

INSTALL COMBINATION STORM DOORS

NORMALLY CONTRACTOR INSTALLED

Combination (windows and screen) storm doors are designed for installation over exterior doors. They are sold almost everywhere, with or without the cost of installation.

Installation

You can save a few dollars (10% to 15% of the purchase price) by installing doors yourself. But you'll need some tools: hammer, drill, screw driver, and weatherstripping. In most cases, it will be easier to have the supplier install your doors himself.

The supplier will first measure all the doors where you want storm doors installed. It will take anywhere from several days to a few weeks to make up your order before the supplier returns to install them. Installation should take less than one-half day.

Before the installer leaves, be sure the doors operate smoothly and close tightly. Check for cracks around the jamb and make sure the seal is as air-tight as possible. Also, remove and replace the exchangeable panels (window and screen) to make sure they fit properly and with a weather tight seal.

Selection: Judging Quality

Door finish: A mill finish (plain aluminum) will oxidize, reducing ease of operation and degrading appearance. An anodized or baked enamel finish is better.

Corner joints: Quality of construction affects the strength and effectiveness of storm doors. Corners are a good place to check construction. They should be strong and air tight. If you can see through the joints, they will leak air.

Weatherstripping: Storm doors are supposed to reduce air leakage around your doors. Weatherstripping quality makes a big difference in how well storm doors can do this. Compare several types before deciding.

Hardware quality: The quality of locks, hinges and catches should be evaluated since it can have a direct effect on durability and is a good indicator of overall construction quality.

Construction material: Storm doors of wood or steel can also be purchased within the same price range as the aluminum variety. They have the same quality differences and should be similarly evaluated. The choice between doors of similar quality but different material is primarily up to your own personal taste.

BUYING INSULATION

From the pages in Part 3 that deal with insulating your house you can get a good idea of what your choice of insulating materials is (see "Materials" at the beginning of each how-to section), how many square feet you need, and whether you need a vapor barrier with your insulation. There are three more things you need to know before you buy:

1. **What the R-Value of the insulation should be** — your money's worth in insulation is measured in R-Value. R-Value is a number that tells you how much resistance the insulation presents to heat flowing through it. The bigger the R-Value, the better the insulation. This page lists recommended R-Values for the different parts of the house.

2. **What kind of insulation to buy** — pages 43 and 44 will help you choose the right kind of insulation for the job you want to do.

3. **How thick your insulation should be** — For the R-Value and type of insulation you're going to buy, look at the table at the bottom of page 44 — it'll tell you how many inches of each type of insulation it takes to achieve the R-Value you need.

NOTE: If you have a choice of insulating materials, and all your choices are available in your area, simply price the same R-Value for both, and get the better buy. Pay more only for more R-Value.

1. What the R-Value of the insulation should be:

UNFINISHED ATTIC, NO FLOOR

Batts, blankets or loose fill in the floor between the joists:

THICKNESS OF EXISTING INSULATION	HOW MUCH TO ADD	HOW MUCH TO ADD IF YOU HAVE ELECTRIC HEAT OR IF YOU HAVE OIL HEAT AND LIVE IN A COLD CLIMATE*	HOW MUCH TO ADD IF YOU HAVE ELECTRIC HEAT AND LIVE IN A COLD CLIMATE**
0"	R-22	R-30	R-38
0"-2"	R-11	R-22	R-30
2"-4"	R-11	R-19	R-22
4"-6"	none	R-11	R-19

*For users of Part 2: add this much if:
— you're doing it yourself and your Heating and Cooling Factors add up to more than 0.4, or
— a contractor is doing it and your Heating and Cooling Factors add up to more than 0.6.

**For users of Part 2: add this much if:
— you're doing it yourself and your Heating and Cooling Factors add up to more than 0.7, or
— a contractor is doing it and your Heating and Cooling Factors add up to more than 1.0.

FINISHED ATTIC

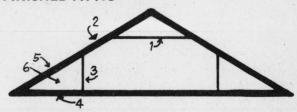

1. Attic Ceiling — see the table at the left under Unfinished Attic, No Floor.
2. Rafters — contractor fills completely with blow-in insulation.
3. Knee Walls — Insulate (5), Outer Attic Rafters instead.
4. Outer Attic Floors — Insulate (5), Outer Attic Rafters instead.
5. Outer Attic Rafters — Add batts or blankets: If there is existing insulation in (3) and (4), add R-11. If there is no existing insulation in (3) and (4), add R-19.
6. End Walls — Add batts or blankets, R-11.

UNFINISHED ATTIC WITH FLOOR

A. Do-it-yourself or Contractor Installed:

Between the collar beams — follow the guidelines above in Unfinished Attic, No Floor.

Rafters and end walls — buy insulation thick enough to fill the space available (usually R-19 for the rafters and R-11 for the end walls).

B. Contractor Installed

Contractor blows loose-fill insulation under the floor. Fill this space completely — see page 42 for the R-Value you should get.

FRAME WALLS — contractor blows in insulation to fill the space inside the walls. See page 42 for the R-Value you should get.

CRAWL SPACE — R-11 batts or blankets against the wall and the edge of the floor.

FLOORS — R-11 batts or blankets between the floor joists, *foil-faced*.

BASEMENT WALLS — R-7 batts or blankets between wall studs. Note: Use R-11 if R-7 is not available.

2. What kind of insulation to buy:

BATTS— glass fiber, rock wool

Where they're used to insulate:
unfinished attic floor
unfinished attic rafters
underside of floors

best suited for standard joist or rafter spacing of 16" or 24", and space between joists relatively free of obstructions

cut in sections 15" or 23" wide, 1" to 7" thick, 4' or 8' long

with or without a vapor barrier backing — if you need one and can't get it, buy polyethylene except that to be used to insulate the underside of floors

easy to handle because of relatively small size

use will result in more waste from trimming sections than use of blankets

fire resistant, moisture resistant

FOAMED IN PLACE— ureaformaldahyde

Where it's used to insulate:
finished frame walls
unfinished attic floor

moisture resistant, fire resistant

may have higher insulating value than blown-in materials

more expensive than blown-in materials

quality of application to date has been very inconsistent — choose a qualified contractor who will guarantee his work.

BLANKETS— glass fiber, rock wool

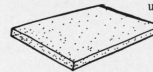

Where they're used to insulate:
unfinished attic floor
unfinished attic rafters
underside of floors

best suited for standard joist or rafter spacing of 16" or 24", and space between joists relatively free of obstructions

cut in sections 15" or 23" wide, 1" to 7" thick in rolls to be cut to length by the installer

with or without a vapor barrier backing

a little more difficult to handle than batts because of size

fire resistant, moisture resistant

RIGID BOARD— extruded polystyrene bead board (expanded polystyrene) urethane board, glass fiber

Where it's used to insulate:
basement wall

NOTE: Polystyrene and urethane rigid board insulation should only be installed by a contractor. They must be covered with 1/2" gypsum wallboard to assure fire safety.

extruded polystyrene and urethane are their own vapor barriers, bead board and glass fiber are not.

high insulating value for relatively small thicknesses, particularly urethane.

comes in 24" or 48" widths

variety of thicknesses from 3/4" to 4"

LOOSE FILL (poured-in) — glass fiber, rock wool, cellulosic fiber, vermiculite, perlite

Where it's used to insulate:

unfinished attic floor

vapor barrier bought and applied separately

best suited for non-standard or irregular joist spacing or when space between joists has many obstructions

glass fiber and rock wool are fire resistant and moisture resistant

cellulosic fiber chemically treated to be fire resistant and moisture resistant; treatment not yet proven to be heat resistant, may break down in a hot attic; check to be sure that bags indicate material meets Federal Specifications. If they do, they'll be clearly labelled.

cellulosic fiber has about 30% more insulation value than rock wool for the same installed thickness (this can be important in walls or under attic floors).

vermiculite is significantly more expensive but can be poured into smaller areas.

vermiculite and perlite have about the same insulating value.

all are easy to install.

LOOSE FILL (blown-in) — glass fiber, rock wool, cellulosic fiber

Where it's used to insulate

unfinished attic floor

finished attic floor

finished frame walls

underside of floors

vapor barrier bought separately

same physical properties as poured-in loose fill.

Because it consists of smaller tufts, cellulosic fiber gets into small nooks and corners more consistently than rock wool or glass fiber when blown into closed spaces such as walls or joist spaces.

When any of these materials are blown into a closed space enough must be blown in to fill the whole space.

3. How thick your insulation should be:

Get the R-Value you need from page 42, and the type of insulation you need from this page and the one before. Use the table below to find out how thick the insulation you buy should be:

TYPE OF INSULATION

	BATTS OR BLANKETS		LOOSE FILL (POURED-IN)			
	glass fiber	rock wool	glass fiber	rock wool	cellulosic fiber	
R-11	3½"-4"	3"	5"	4"	3"	R-11
R-19	6"-6½"	5¼"	8"-9"	6"-7"	5"	R-19
R-22	6½"	6"	10"	7"-8"	6"	R-22
R-30	9½"-10½"*	9"*	13"-14"	10"-11"	8"	R-30
R-38	12"-13"*	10½"*	17"-18"	13"-14"	10"-11"	R-38

* two batts or blankets required.

INSULATE YOUR UNFINISHED ATTIC

AN EASY DO-IT-YOURSELF PROJECT

Install batts or blankets between the joists or trusses in your attic

OR

Pour in loose fill between the joists or trusses

OR

Lay in batts or pour in loose fill over existing insulation if you've decided you don't have enough already. *Don't* add a vapor barrier if you're installing additional insulation.

NOTE: If your attic has trusses in it, this section still applies — the insulation goes in the same place, but job is more difficult.

Tools

1. Temporary lighting
2. Temporary flooring
3. Duct or masking tape (2" wide)
4. Heavy duty staple gun and staples, or hammer and tacks
5. Heavy duty shears or linoleum knife to cut batts or blankets and plastic for vapor barrier

Safety

1. Provide good lighting
2. Lay boards or plywood sheets down over the tops of the joists or trusses to form a walkway (the ceiling below won't support your weight).
3. Be careful of roofing nails protruding through roof sheathing.
4. If you use glass fiber or mineral wool, wear gloves and breathing mask, and keep the material wrapped until you're ready to put it in place.

Materials

What you'll need

Batts, glass fiber or rock wool

Blankets, glass fiber or rock wool

Loose fill, rock wool, cellulosic fiber, or vermiculite

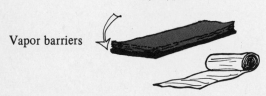

Vapor barriers

How much

(a) Accurately determine your attic area.

If necessary, divide it into rectangles and sum the areas.

$$\underline{\hspace{2cm}} \times \underline{\hspace{2cm}} = \underline{\hspace{2cm}}$$
$$\underline{\hspace{2cm}} \times \underline{\hspace{2cm}} = \underline{\hspace{2cm}}$$
$$\underline{\hspace{2cm}} \times \underline{\hspace{2cm}} = \underline{\hspace{2cm}}$$
$$\text{Total} = \underline{\hspace{2cm}}$$

(b) Insulation area = (.9) X (total) = \underline{\hspace{2cm}}

(c) Vapor barrier area (see if you need one — page 52).
  1. Batts or blankets with vapor barrier backing — use insulation area.
  2. Polyethylene (for use with loose fill, or if backed batts or blankets are not available) —use insulation area, but plan on waste since the polyethylene will be installed in strips between the joists or trusses, and you may not be able to cut an even number of strips out of a roll.

(d) Insulation thickness — see page 42. If page 42 calls for R-30 or more, you may be adding two layers of insulation. Lay the first layer between the joists, and the second layer across the joists. (This is very difficult with trusses — lay the second layer parallel to the trusses, or even better, — use loose fill.) Figure attic area for the second layer.

Installation

Preparation

Put in temporary lighting and flooring, check for leaks and check need for ventilation and vapor barrier (see page 52). Seal all places where pipes or wires penetrate the attic floor. **NOTE:** Some manufacturers may recommend using polyethylene in a continuous sheet across the joists or trusses. If you aren't adding insulation that covers the tops of these framing members with at least 3½" of insulation, laying a continuous sheet may cause condensation along them; lay strips as shown instead.

1

Install temporary flooring and lights. Keep insulation in wrappers until you are ready to install. It comes wrapped in a compressed state and expands when the wrappers are removed.

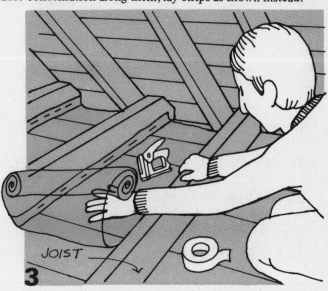

3

Install separate vapor barrier if needed (see page 52). Lay in polyethylene strips between joists or trusses. Staple or tack in place. Seal seams and holes with tape. (Seams may be overlapped 6" instead.)

2

Check for roof leaks, looking for water stains or marks. If you find leakage, make repairs before you insulate. Wet insulation is ineffective and can damage the structure of your home.

4

If you're using loose fill, install baffles at the inside of the eave vents so that the insulation won't block the flow of air from the vents into the attic. Be sure that insulation extends out far enough to cover the top plate.

Installing the insulation

Either lay in batts or blankets between the joists or pour in loose fill. If you're using batts or blankets with a vapor barrier, place the barrier on the side toward the living area.

5 Lay in blankets or batts between joists or trusses. (Note: batts and blankets are slightly wider than joist spacing so they'll fit snugly). If blankets are used, cut long runs first to conserve material, using leftovers for shorter spaces. Slide insulation under wiring wherever possible.

7 The space between the chimney and the wood framing should be filled with *non-combustible* material, preferably unfaced batts or blankets. Also, the National Electric Code requires that insulation be kept 3" away from light fixtures.

OR

6 Pour in loose fill insulation between the joists up to the top of the joists. Use a board or garden rake to level it. Fill all the nooks and crannies but don't cover recessed light fixtures or exhaust fans.

8 Cut ends of batts or blankets to fit snugly around cross bracing. Cut the next batt in a similar way to allow the ends to butt tightly together. If page 42 calls for an R-Value that requires a second layer, place it **at right angles** to the joists.

INSULATE YOUR UNFINISHED FLOORED ATTIC

TWO OPTIONS AVAILABLE

1. **CONTRACTOR INSTALLED:** blow-in insulation under the flooring and between the joists.
2. **DO IT YOURSELF OR CONTRACTOR:** install batts between the rafters, collar beams, and the studs on the end walls.

CONTRACTOR INSTALLED

Types of materials contractors use

Blown-in insulation
   glass fiber
   rock wool
   cellulosic fiber

Preparation

Do you need ventilation in your attic? See page 52.

Check for roof leaks, looking for water stains or marks. If you can find any leaks, make repairs before you insulate. Wet insulation is useless and can damage the structure of your house.

What your contractor will do

The insulation is installed by blowing the insulating material under air pressure through a big flexible hose into the spaces between the attic floor and the ceiling of the rooms below. Bags of insulating material are fed into a blowing machine that mixes the insulation with air and forces it through the hose and into place. Before starting

the machine, the contractor will locate the cross bracing between the joists in the attic. He'll then remove the floor boards above the cross bracing and install the insulation by blowing it in on each side of the cross bracing to make sure there are no spaces left unfilled. Since there's no effective way to partially fill a space, all of the spaces should be completely filled to ensure proper coverage. Normally the job will take no longer than a day.

What you should check

First be very careful about choosing a contractor. See page 64 for advice on how to make a selection.

Before you sign an agreement with your contractor, decide how much and what kind of insulation you're buying and make sure it's included in the contract. Insulation material properly installed will achieve a single insulating value (R-Value) for the depth of your joist space. You should agree on what that insulating value is with the contractor, before the job begins. Next check a bag of the type of insulation he intends to use. On it, there will be a table which will indicate how many square feet of attic floor that bag is meant to cover while achieving the desired insulating value. The information may be in different forms (number of square feet per bag or number of bags per 1000 square feet), so you may have to do some simple division to use the number correctly. Knowing this and the area of your attic, you should be able to figure out how many bags must be installed to give you the desired R-Value. This number should be agreed upon between you and the contractor before the job is begun. While the job is in progress, be sure the right amount is being installed. There's nothing wrong with having the contractor save the empty bags so that you can count them (5 bags more or less than the amount you agreed on is an acceptable difference from the estimate).

After the job is finished, it's a good idea to drill 1/4" diameter holes in the floor about a foot apart. This will help prevent condensation from collecting under the floor in winter.

DO-IT-YOURSELF

Install batts or blankets in your attic between the rafters and collar beams, and the studs on the end walls.

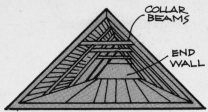

This measure will involve installing 2x4 beams which span between each roof rafter at ceiling height, if your attic doesn't already have them. This gives you a ventilation space above for the insulation (see page 52).

NOTE: The materials, methods, and thicknesses of insulation are the same for both do-it-yourself and contractor jobs. For advice on choosing a contractor, see page 64.

Safety

1. Provide good lighting
2. Be careful of roofing nails protruding through the roof sheathing
3. If you use glass fiber or mineral wool, wear gloves and a breathing mask and keep the material wrapped until you're about to use it

Tools

1. Temporary lighting
2. Heavy duty staple gun and staples
3. Linoleum knife or heavy duty shears to cut the insulation
4. Duct or masking tape (2" wide)
5. Hammer, nails (only if you're putting in collar beams)
6. Power or hand saw (only if you're putting in collar beams)

Materials

What you'll need

Buy either batts or blankets, made out of glass fiber or rock wool.

Do you need insulation with an attached vapor barrier? Follow the guidelines on page 52.

Exception: For the area between the collar beams, if you're laying the new insulation on top of old insulation, buy insulation without a vapor barrier if possible, or slash the vapor barrier on the new insulation.

How Thick?

1. For the area between the collar beams, follow the guidelines on page 42. ("Existing insulation" means either insulation between the collar beams or in the attic floor.)

2. For the rafters and end walls, buy insulation that's thick enough to fill up the rafter and stud spaces. If there's some existing insulation in there, the combined thickness of the new and old insulation together should fill up the spaces.

How much

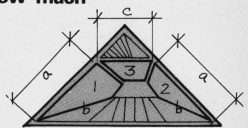

1. Figure out the area you want the insulation to cover between your rafters and collar beams (shown above). In general, figure each area to be covered, and add the areas up. If your attic is like the one shown, measure distances a, b, and c, enter them below, and do the figuring indicated (the .9 allows for the space taken up by rafters or collar beams.):

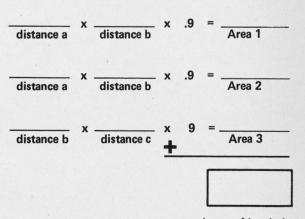

$$\underline{\hspace{2cm}} \times \underline{\hspace{2cm}} \times .9 = \underline{\hspace{2cm}}$$
distance a   distance b   Area 1

$$\underline{\hspace{2cm}} \times \underline{\hspace{2cm}} \times .9 = \underline{\hspace{2cm}}$$
distance a   distance b   Area 2

$$\underline{\hspace{2cm}} \times \underline{\hspace{2cm}} \times 9 = \underline{\hspace{2cm}}$$
distance b   distance c   Area 3

total area of insulation
needed for rafters
collar beams.

2. Calculate the length of 2x4 stock you'll need for collar beams. Measure the length of span you need between rafters (c) and count the number of collar beams you need to install. Multiply to get the length of stock you need. You can have the lumber yard cut it to length at a small charge. If you cut it yourself, allow for waste. If you plan to finish your attic, check with your lumber yard to make sure 2" X 4" 's are strong enough to support the ceiling you plan to install.

3. Figure out the area of each end wall you want to insulate. Measure (d) and (e) and multiply to determine the area. Multiply by (.9) to correct for the space taken up by the studs, then multiply by the number of end walls.

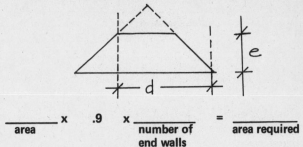

$$\underline{\hspace{2cm}}_{\text{area}} \times\ .9\ \times \underline{\hspace{2cm}}_{\substack{\text{number of} \\ \text{end walls}}} = \underline{\hspace{2cm}}_{\text{area required}}$$

Installation

Preparation

Check for roof leaks, looking for water stains or marks. If you can find any leaks, make repairs before you insulate. Wet insulation is useless and can damage the structure of your house. Determine your need for more ventilation by referring to page 52. Put up your temporary lights and:

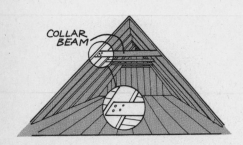

1. Install 2x4 collar beams spanning from rafter to rafter at the ceiling height you want. Every pair of rafters should have a collar beam spanning between them.

   Note: If you're installing new insulation over existing insulation:

   Between the Rafters and Between the End Wall Studs, cut the old insulation loose where it has been stapled, push it to the back of the cavities, and slash the old vapor barrier (if any) before you lay the new insulation over it.

   Between the Collar Beams, lay the new insulation above the old. Lay it over the tops of the collar beams in an unbroken layer at right angles to the beams. Use insulation that does not have a vapor barrier for this part of the job. If you can't get insulation without a vapor barrier, slash the vapor barrier before laying it down, so that moisture won't get trapped in the insulation.

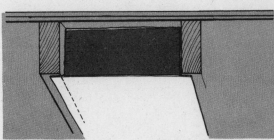

2. Install batts or blanket sections in place between the rafters and collar beams. Install with the vapor barrier on the inside, the side toward you. Don't try to use a continuous length of insulation where the collar beams meet the rafters. It will only result in gaps that are very hard to fill. Install batts in the end walls the same way. Be sure to trim carefully to fit the angles on the end walls.

3. Install batts or blanket sections by stapling the facing flange to the *edge* of the rafter or collar beam. Don't staple to the outside of the rafters; the vapor barrier will have a break at every rafter; and you may compress the insulation against the sheathing, reducing its insulating value.

INSULATE YOUR FINISHED ATTIC

TWO OPTIONS AVAILABLE

(and worth considering if there's under 4 inches of insulation already there.)

1. **Contractor Installation:** insulation blown into the ceiling, sloping rafters and outer attic floors; batts installed in the knee walls.

2. **Do-it-yourself:** installation of batts, blankets or loose fill in all attic spaces you can get to.

Where the insulation needs to be installed

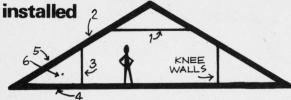

1. Attic Ceiling
2. Rafters
3. Knee Walls
4. Outer Attic Floors, or
5. Outer Attic Rafters
6. End Walls

CONTRACTOR INSTALLED
Types of materials contractors use

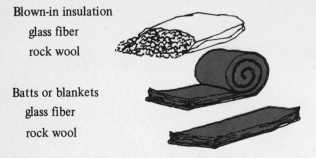

Blown-in insulation
   glass fiber
   rock wool

Batts or blankets
   glass fiber
   rock wool

Preparation

How thick should the insulation be? See page 42.

Check your need for ventilation and a vapor barrier. See page 52.

Check for roof leaks, looking for water stains or marks. If you can find any leaks, make repairs before you insulate. Wet insulation is useless and can damage the structure of your house.

What your contractor will do

Your contractor will blow insulation into the open joist spaces above your attic ceiling, between the rafters, and into the floor of the outer attic space, then install batts in the knee walls. If you want to keep the outer attic spaces heated for storage or any other purpose, you should have the contractor install batts between the outer attic rafters instead of insulating the outer floors and knee walls.

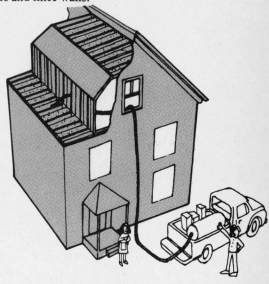

Page 48 describes how blown-in insulation is installed under an unfinished attic floor. This process is much the same for open joists with no floor over them. Pages 49-50 describe the right way to install batts.

DO-IT-YOURSELF

You can insulate wherever you can get into the unfinished spaces.

Installing insulation in your attic ceiling is the same as installing it in an unfinished attic. Look at pages 45-47 to see how this is done.

If you want to insulate your outer attic spaces yourself, install batts between the rafters and the studs in the small triangular end walls. Look at page 50 to see how to do this.

DO YOU NEED A VAPOR BARRIER OR MORE VENTILATION IN YOUR ATTIC?

CONTRACTOR INSTALLED OR DO-IT-YOURSELF

Whenever you add insulation to your house, you should consider the need for a vapor barrier or more ventilation where you're doing the work.

A vapor barrier will prevent water vapor from condensing and collecting in your new insulation or on the beams and rafters of your house.

Added ventilation will remove water vapor before it gets a chance to condense and will also increase summer comfort by cooling off your attic.

What you need

If you're insulating your attic and:

. . . you live in Zone I

1. Install a vapor barrier (unless you are blowing insulation into a finished attic)

2. Add ventilation area equal to 1/300 your attic floor area if:

    Signs of condensation occur after one heating season

    OR

    You can't install a vapor barrier with your insulation

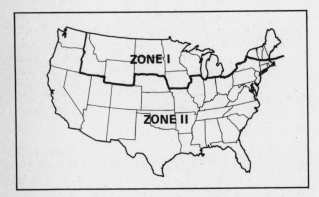

. . . if you live in Zone II and don't have air conditioning

1. Install a vapor barrier toward the living space if you are insulating a finished attic (with other attics a vapor barrier is optional).

2. Add ventilation area equal to 1/300 your attic floor area if signs of condensation occur after one heating season.

. . . you live in Zone II and have air conditioning

1. Install a vapor barrier toward the living space if you are insulating a finished attic (with other attics a vapor barrier is optional).

2. Add ventilation area equal to 1/150 your attic floor area.

What should be installed

Vapor barriers: If you are installing batt or blanket insulation, and you need a vapor barrier, buy the batts or blankets with the vapor barrier attached. Install them with the vapor barrier side toward the living space.

If you are installing a loose fill insulation, lay down polyethylene (heavy, clear plastic) in strips between the joists first.

DON'T BLOCK VENTILATION PATH

Ventilation: Install ventilation louvers (round or rectangular) in the eaves and gables (ridge vents are also available but are more difficult and costly to install in your house). The total open area of these louvers should be either 1/300 or 1/150 of your attic area (see "What You Need" above), and evenly divided between the gables and the eaves.

Ventilation louvers should be installed by a carpenter unless you are an experienced handyman.

Don't Block Ventilation Path with Insulation.

INSULATE YOUR WOOD FRAME WALLS

CONTRACTOR INSTALLED

Normally, insulating material is blown into the spaces in a wood frame wall through holes drilled from the outside or the inside. An alternate procedure uses plastic foam (ureaformaldahyde) to fill the stud spaces.

NOTE: Condensation in insulated walls may be a problem; see box on condensation, p.19.

Types of materials contractors use

Blow-in insulation:

glass fiber

rock wool

cellulosic fiber

Foam-in insulation:

plastic foam installed as a foam under slight pressure which hardens to form insulation. Quality of application to date has been very inconsistent — ask your local HUD/FHA office to recommend a qualified installer.

What your contractor will do

The contractor will measure the area you want insulated to determine how much material he will need and to estimate the cost. To install the insulation, the contractor must be able to get all the spaces in the wall. For each space he must drill a hole, usually in the outside wall, after removing the finished layer (usually clapboard or shingle). This always amounts to a lot of holes, but once the job is complete, a good contractor will leave no traces behind.

If you have brick veneer on the exterior, the procedure is much the same, except that it may be cheaper to do it from the inside.

Once the holes in the wall have been made your contractor is then ready to install the insulation. If the insulation is blow-in insulation he'll be following the process outlined on page 48. If he's using foam, he'll pump the foam into the wall spaces through a flexible hose with an applicator. With either method, each space will be completely filled, and the siding replaced.

What you should check

First be very careful about selecting a contractor. See page 64 for advice on how to make a choice.

Before you sign an agreement with your contractor, define what you're buying and make sure it's spelled out in the contract. Insulation material properly installed will add an R-Value of 8 for rock wool, 10 for cellulosic fiber, or 11.5 for ureaformaldehyde in a standard wood frame wall. You should agree on what that R-Value is with the contractor before the job begins. Next, check a bag of the type of insulation he intends to use (there will only be bags of mineral fiber or cellulosic fiber — there's no good way to check quantity with foam). On it, there will be a table which will indicate how many square feet of wall space that bag is meant to fill while giving your house the desired R value. The information may be in different forms (number of square feet per bag or number of bags per 1000 square feet), so you may have to do some simple division to use the number correctly.

Knowing this and the area of your walls, you should be able to figure out about how many bags should be installed to give you the desired R-value.

This number should be agreed upon between you and the contractor before the job is begun. While the job is in progress be sure the correct amount is being installed. There's nothing wrong with having the contractor save the empty bags so you can count them — 4 or 5 bags more or less than the amount you agreed on is an acceptable difference from the estimate.

INSULATE YOUR CRAWL SPACE WALLS

Tools

1. Hammer and nails
2. Heavy duty shears or linoleum knife
3. Temporary lighting
4. Portable fan or blower to provide ventilation
5. Tape measure
6. Duct or Masking Tape (2" wide)

Materials
What you'll need

1. R11 (3-3½" thick) blankets of rock wool or glass fiber; without a vapor barrier

2. Six mil polyethylene plastic to lay on earth for vapor barrier (mil's are a measure of thickness)

3. 1/2" X 1-1/2" stock for nailing strips at the sill and at the band joist.

TWO OPTIONS AVAILABLE

(1) **Do-It-Yourself:** Install batt or blanket insulation around the walls and perimeter of your crawl space. Lay a plastic vapor barrier down on the crawl space earth.

(2) **Contractor Installed:** If your crawl space presents access or working space problems, you may want to consider having a contractor do the work for you. The contractor will probably follow a method similar to the do-it-yourself method described below. But if he suggests something different, have him price both methods and show you which is better. See page 64 for advice on how to select a contractor.

> **NOTE:** The method of insulation shown here should not be used by residents of Alaska, Minnesota, and northern Maine. The extreme frost penetration in these areas can cause heaving of the foundation if the insulation method shown here is used. Residents of these areas should contact local HUD/FHA field offices for advice.

Safety

1. Provide adequate temporary lighting
2. Wear gloves and a breathing mask when working with glass fiber or rock wool
3. Provide adequate ventilation
4. Keep lights, fan, and all wires well off wet ground

How much

1. Determine area to be insulated; measure the length and average height of the wall to be insulated; add 3' to the height (for perimeter insulation) and multiply the two to find total insulation area

(length) X (height + 3') = area

_____ X _____ + 3' = _____

2. Determine the area to be covered by the vapor barrier by finding the area of your crawl space

(length) X (width) = area

_____ X _____ = _____

You may have to divide your crawl space into several rectangles — measure them and add up the areas.

(length)	X	(width)	=
_____	X	_____	= _____
_____	X	_____	= _____
_____	X	_____	= _____
		TOTAL	=

3. The total length of nailing strips required equals the length of wall to be insulated

Installation

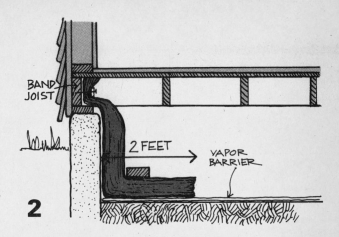

Drawing 1: Where the joists run at right angles to the wall, press short pieces of insulation against the Header — they should fit snugly. Then install the wall and perimeter insulation by nailing the top of each strip to the Sill using the 1/2" X 1-1/2" nailers. Make sure the batts fit snugly against each other, and that you cut them long enough to cover 2 feet of floor as in Drawing 2.

Drawing 2: Where the joists run parallel to the wall, you don't need the short pieces of insulation, just install the wall and perimeter insulation by nailing the top of each strip to the Band Joist, using the 1/2" X 1-1/2" nailers.

When all batts have been installed, lay down the polyethylene vapor barrier, tucking it under the batts all the way to the foundation wall. Tape the joints of the vapor barrier or lap them at least 6". Finally lay 2 X 4 lumber along the wall on top of the batts to weight the batts in place. (Rocks work well, too.) Plan your work to minimize stepping or crawling on the vapor barrier.

VENTILATING YOUR CRAWL SPACE

Even with a plastic vapor barrier on the floor, the air in your crawl space will be too damp if fresh air doesn't get in there from time to time. This will mean your new insulation will be wet, and it won't keep your house as warm. It will also mean that wooden members that hold up your house will be wet, and they'll rot. Proper ventilation will prevent both of these problems:

1. If your crawl space is part of your forced-air heating system (in other words, if air from your furnace moves through it), seal your crawl space as tightly as possible--- the air moving through it from your furnace is enough ventilation in winter. If you have crawl space vents, keep them shut in winter, open in summer. If there are no vents, run the blower on your furnace 3 or 4 times during the summer to keep the air in the crawl space from getting too damp.

2. All other crawl spaces should have vents in them that can be opened in summer (to clear out the damp air), and closed **tightly** in winter to make the most of your new insulation. You can make a cover for them to install in winter. Note: Your furnace may get its combustion air from the crawl space. If so, some of the vents should be left open. Check with your local HUD/FHA office.

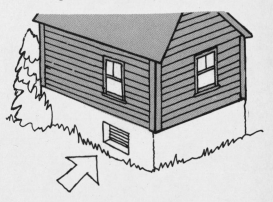

INSULATE YOUR FLOOR

TWO OPTIONS AVAILABLE

1. DO-IT-YOURSELF

Install batts or blankets between the floor joists by stapling wire mesh or chicken wire to the bottom of the joists and sliding the batts or blankets in on top of the wire. Place vapor barrier up.

The job is quite easy to do in most cases. If you are insulating over a crawl space there may be some problems with access or working room, but careful planning can make things go much more smoothly and easily.

Check your floor joist spacing — this method will work best with standard 16" or 24" joist spacing. If you have non-standard or irregular spacing there will be more cutting and fitting and some waste of material.

2. CONTRACTOR INSTALLED

See page 57.

DO-IT-YOURSELF
Tools

1. Heavy duty shears or linoleum knife

2. Temporary lighting with waterproof wiring and connectors

3. Portable fan or blower to provide ventilation

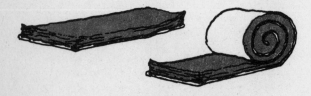

4. Tape measure

5. Heavy duty staple gun and staples

Safety

1. Provide adequate temporary lighting

2. Wear gloves and breathing mask when working with glass fiber or rock wool

3. Provide adequate ventilation

4. Keep lights and all wires off wet ground

Materials
What you'll need

1. R11 (3"-3½") batts or blankets or rock wool or glass fiber, preferably with foil facing (See Installation).

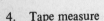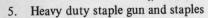

2. Wire mesh or chicken wire of convenient width for handling in tight space.

How much

Determine the area to be insulated by measuring the length and width and multiplying to get the area.

(length) X (width) = area

(_____) X (_____) = _____

You may find it necessary to divide the floor into smaller areas and add them.

(length) X (width) = area

(_____) X (_____) = _____

(_____) X (_____) = _____

(_____) X (_____) = _____ +

total area = _____

(.9)(total area) = area of insulation

(.9)(_____) = _____

total area = area of wire mesh or chicken wire

Installation

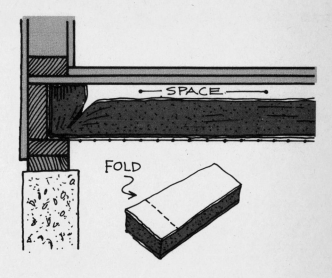

Start at a wall at one end of the joists and work out. Staple the wire to the bottom of the joists, and at right angles to them. Slide batts in on top of the wire. Work with short sections of wire and batts so that it won't be too difficult to get the insulation in place. Plan sections to begin and end at obstructions such as cross bracing.

Buy insulation with a vapor barrier, and install the vapor barrier facing up (next to the warm side) leaving an air space between the vapor barrier and the floor. Get foil-faced insulation if you can; it will make the air space insulate better. Be sure that ends of batts fit snugly up against the bottom of the floor to prevent loss of heat up end. Don't block combustion air openings for furnaces.

INSULATE YOUR BASEMENT WALLS

EXTERIOR WALLS ONLY

A MODERATELY EASY DO-IT-YOURSELF PROJECT

Install 2" X 3" studs along the walls to be insulated. Add glass fiber blanket insulation between the furring strips and finish with wallboard or panelling.

> **NOTE:** The method of insulation shown here should not be used by residents of Alaska, Minnesota, and northern Maine. The extreme frost penetration in these areas can cause heaving of the foundation if the insulation method shown here is used. Residents of these areas should contact local HUD/FHA field offices for advice.

Tools

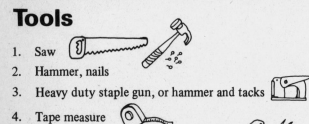

1. Saw
2. Hammer, nails
3. Heavy duty staple gun, or hammer and tacks
4. Tape measure
5. Linoleum knife or heavy duty shears
6. Level
7. Small sledge hammer, masonry nails

Safety

1. Provide adequate temporary lighting

2. If you use glass fiber or rock wool, wear gloves and a breathing mask, and keep the material wrapped until you are ready to use it

Materials

What you'll need

1. R7 (2-2½ inch) Batt or blanket insulation, glass fiber or rockwool, with a vapor barrier (buy polyethylene if you can't get batts or blankets with a vapor barrier)

2. 2" X 3" studs

3. Drywall or panelling

4. Waterproof paint, if necessary

How much

1. Find the average height above the ground of the walls you intend to insulate and add two feet. Then measure the length of the walls you intend to insulate. Multiply the two figures to determine how many square feet of insulation is needed.

   (height) X (length) = area

   _____ X _____ = _____

2. Find the linear feet of studs you'll need by multiplying the length of the walls you intend to insulate by (6).

   (6) X (length) = (linear ft.)

   (6) X _____ = _____

3. The area of wall covering equals the basement wall height times the length of wall you intend to finish.

   (height) X (length) = area

   _____ X _____ = _____

Installation

Preparation

Check to see whether or not moisture is coming through your basement walls from the ground outside. If it is and your walls are damp, you should eliminate the cause of the dampness to prevent the insulation you're going to install from becoming wet and ineffective.

Nail the bottom plate to the floor at the base of the wall with a hammer and concrete nails. Install studs 16 or 24 inches apart after the top plate is nailed to the joists above. (Where the wall runs parallel to the joists, nail the top plate to the tops of the studs, and fasten the studs to the wall.)

Cut blankets into sections long enough to extend from the top plate to 2 feet below the ground line. Staple them into place between the studs, with the vapor barrier towards the living space. **NOTE:** in northern climates there will be added benefit to installing the insulation the full height of the wall.

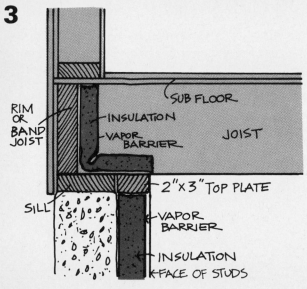

Install another small piece of insulation above the furring and against the sill to insulate the sill and band joist.

Install finish wall board or panelling over insulation and furring.

SAVING ENERGY WITH YOUR HEATING, AIR CONDITIONING & WATER HEATING

TWO OPTIONS AVAILABLE

1. **Routine Servicing** — your serviceman should check all your heating and cooling equipment and do any needed maintenance once a year.

2. **Repair or Replacement** — some of your heating and cooling equipment may be so badly worn or outmoded that it will pay you to replace it now and get your money back in a few years.

Routine Servicing

A periodic checkup and maintenance of your heating and cooling equipment can reduce your fuel consumption by about 10 per cent. Locating a good heating/cooling specialist and sticking with him is a good way to ensure that your equipment stays in top fuel-saving condition. Your local fuel supplier or heating/cooling system repair specialist are the people to call — you can find them in the Yellow Pages under:

Heating Contractors   Electric Heating
Air Conditioning Equipment   Oil Burner-Equipment
Furnaces-Heating   and Service

Check out the people you contact with the Better Business Bureau and other homeowners in your area. Once you're satisfied you're in touch with a reputable outfit, a *service contract* is the best arrangement to make. For an annual fee, this gets you a periodic tuneup of your heating/cooling system, and insures you against repairs of most components. A regular arrangement like this is the best one — the serviceman gets to know your system, and you're assured of regular maintenance from a company you know.

In this section, there are lists of items your serviceman should check for each type of heating or cooling system. Some items may vary from brand to brand, but *go over the list with your serviceman*. Also listed here are service items you can probably take care of yourself and save even more money. If you don't want to service your system yourself, *make sure* you add those items to your serviceman's list.

Repair or Replacement

. . . of your equipment may be necessary.

When you are faced with major repairs, inevitably the question comes up: should we fix what we've got, or buy new equipment? It's an important question but not difficult to answer if you consider the right things:

1. Get several estimates — the larger the job the more estimates. The special knowledge of the equipment dealer and installer is most needed here — they'll study your house, measure the walls and windows, and should give you *written* estimates.

2. Check to see what your fuel costs are now. See page 25 to estimate your heating bill if it's mixed in with other utilities.

3. Ask each contractor who gives you an estimate to tell you how many years he thinks it will take before the amount you save by having the new system equals what you paid for it. Remember, fuel costs are going up.

Furnace Maintenance

OIL BURNER

Every Year

Adjust and clean burner unit

Adjust fuel-to-air ratio for maximum efficiency

Check for oil leaks

Check electrical connections, especially on safety devices

Clean heating elements and surfaces

Adjust dampers and draft regulator

Change oil filters

Change air filter

Change oil burner nozzle

Check oil pump

Clean house thermostat contacts and adjust

There are several tests servicemen can use to check oil furnace efficiency:

Draft Test to see if heat is being lost up the chimney or if draft is not enough to properly burn your oil.

Smoke Test to see if your oil is being burned cleanly and completely.

CO_2 test to see if fuel is being burned completely.

Stack Temperature Test to see if stack gases are too hot or not hot enough.

COAL FURNACE

At the end of each heating season

Adjust and clean stoker

Clean burner of all coal, ash and clinkers

Oil the inside of the coal screw and hopper to prevent rust

GAS FURNACE (bottled, LP or natural)

Every 3 Years

Check operation of main gas valve, pressure regulator, and safety control valve

Adjust primary air supply nozzle for proper combustion

Clean thermostat contacts and adjust for proper operation

See Draft Test and Stack Temperature Test above

ELECTRIC FURNACE

Very little maintenance required. Check the manufacturers specifications.

Heat Distribution Systems

Some items here you can do yourself to keep your system at top efficiency. For the ones you can't, check above on how to pick a serviceman. Note: except where it says otherwise, these are all once a year items.

HOT WATER HEATING SYSTEM

Serviceman:

Check pump operation

Check operation of flow control valve

Check for piping leaks

Check operation of radiator valves

Drain and Flush the boiler

Oil Pump Motor

You can do this yourself:

Bleed air from the system. Over time, a certain amount of air will creep into the pipes in your system. It will find its way to the radiators at the top of your house, and wherever there's air, it keeps out hot water. There's usually a small valve at the top of each radiator. *Once or twice a year* open the valve at each radiator. Hold a bucket under it, and keep the valve open until the water comes out. Watch out, the water is *hot*.

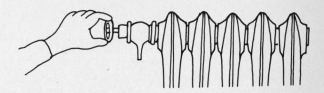

Draining and Flushing the boiler is also something you can do yourself. Ask your serviceman to show you how.

FORCED HOT AIR HEATING SYSTEM

Once a Year

Serviceman:

Check blower operation

Oil the blower motor if it doesn't have sealed bearings.

Check for duct leaks where duct is accessible.

You can do these yourself:

Clean or replace air filters — *this is important,* easy to do, and is something that needs to be done more often than it pays to have a serviceman do it. Every 30 to 60 days during the heating season you should clean or replace (depending on whether they're disposable) the air filters near the furnace in your system. Ask your serviceman how to do it, buy a supply, and stick to a schedule — you can save a lot of fuel this way.

Clean the fan blade that moves the air through your system — it gets dirty easily and won't move the air well unless it's clean. Do this every year.

Keep all registers clean — Vacuum them every few weeks. Warm air coming out of the registers should have a free path unobstructed by curtains or furniture.

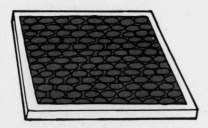

STEAM HEAT SYSTEM

With steam heat, if your serviceman checks your burner, (see Furnace Maintenance above) and the water system in your boiler, most of his work is done. There are two things you can do to save energy, though:

Insulate steam pipes that are running through spaces you don't want to heat.

Every 3 weeks during the heating season, drain a bucket of water out of your boiler (your serviceman will show you how) — this keeps sediment off the bottom of the boiler. If the sediment is allowed to stay there, it will actually *insulate* your boiler from the flame in your burner and a lot of heat will go up the chimney that would have heated your home.

Whole-House Air Conditioning

Once a Year

(Got room air conditioners? – many of these hints apply, ask your dealer about what you can do to your room air conditioners)

Serviceman:

Oil bearings on fan and compressor if they are not sealed

Measure electrical current drawn by compressor

Check pulley belt tension

Check for refrigerating fluid leaks and add fluid if needed

Check electrical connections

Re-adjust dampers — if your air conditioner uses the same ducts as your heating system, different settings are usually required for summer cooling than for winter heating.

Flush evaporator drain line.

You Can Do These Yourself

Clean or replace air filters — *this is important,* and if done every 30 to 60 days will save you far more money in fuel than the cost of the filters.

Clean the condenser coils of dust, grass clippings, etc.

NOTE: **Your condenser is the part of your air conditioner that sits outside your house. It should be shaded — if it has to work in the sun it wastes a lot of fuel. When you shade it, make sure you don't obstruct the flow of air out and around it.**

Buying a room air conditioner? — see Part 4.

Water Heaters

Once a Year

Serviceman:

Adjust damper (for gas or oil)

Adjust burner and clean burner surfaces (for oil)

Check electrodes (for electric)

De-lime tank

You can do this yourself:

Once or twice a year, drain a bucket of water out of the bottom of the heater tank — sometimes it's full of

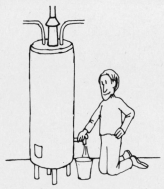

sediment. The sediment *insulates* the water in the tank from the burner flame — *that* wastes energy.

This is important: Don't set your water heater any higher than you need to — your heater burns fuel

keeping your water hot when you're not using it — the higher you set it, the more it burns. If you've got a

dishwasher, *140°* is high enough — if not, *120°* is plenty. Depending on the type of fuel you use, this simple setback will save you $5 to $45 a year. (You say your heater says HIGH, MED, LOW? — Call your dealer and ask him which setting means 140 or 120 degrees.) Note: settings over 140° can shorten the life of water heaters, especially those that are glass-lined.

More about hot water conservation — See Part 4.

Duct Insulation

If the ducts for either your heating or your air conditioning system run exposed through your attic or garage (or any other space that is not heated or cooled) they should be insulated. Duct insulation comes generally in blankets 1 or 2" thick. Get the thicker variety, particularly if you've got rectangular ducts. If you're doing this job at all, it's worth it to do it right. For air conditioning ducts, make sure you get the kind of insulation that has a vapor barrier (the vapor barrier goes on the outside). Seal the joints of the insulation tightly with tape to avoid condensation.

NOTE: Check for leaks in the duct and tape them tightly before insulating.

CHOOSING A CONTRACTOR

If you decide that a particular home improvement you want to make should be done by a contractor, there are some things you should know about finding the right person for the job. The large majority of contractors take pride in their business, are conscientious, and honest. But you should still spend some time and effort in making your choice, and once the choice is made, in clearly defining the job.

1. Where to start looking

Yellow Pages under "Insulation Contractors — Cold and Heat." Don't be suspicious of the small operation — even just a carpenter and his helper. You're doing a relatively small project and often the small business man will give you an excellent job.

Local Chapter of the National Association of Home Builders or Home Builders Association. They will be very helpful in recommending contractors.

Your banker. It's in his interest to recommend a man who will do a good job if he's loaning you the money to do the work.

Local government offices for government funded or non-profit operated home improvement assistance centers. They don't exist everywhere but the ones that do are interested in helping, and maintain files on contractors that they recommend.

From these sources, establish a list of three or four contractors from which to select.

2. How to select from your list

Ask each contractor for a list of past customers, and check their satisfaction with his work.

See how long each contractor has been in business — in general, the longer the better.

Call your local Better Business Bureau and ask if there have been any complaints against each of the contractors on your list.

Get estimates from each on any job you think will cost more than $200.00.

3. Once you've selected a contractor — put it IN WRITING

Have him write up a specific contract for your job.

Check the contract carefully for work content and warranty. The best way to do this is to make a list of all the things you feel he should do in the course of the job (use the applicable Part III pages for assistance here). Then check what you know should be included against what's in the contract.

Sign the contract only when you are fully satisfied that it details everything you want done. Insisting on a detailed contract doesn't mean that you don't trust your contractor. But once you have a contract, each of you knows his limit of responsibility before the job begins.

GETTING FINANCING

If you don't want to pay for your energy fix-up program out of your savings, and you want to get a much better interest rate than either a loan on your credit card or refinancing your present home mortgage will give you, try one of these:

Where to Get Financing (and Information)	What Kind of Financing	How Long to Repay
Commercial Bank Savings and Loan Mutual Savings Bank	1. Home Improvement Loan	2-4 years
	2. FHA/HUD Title I	12 years (this is a recent increase from 7 years)
	NOTE: Lenders are not allowed to charge fees of any kind of this type of loan, and the maximum permissable amount that can be made under Title I has just been increased from $5,000 to $10,000.	
Your Credit Union	Depends on the Credit Union, but usually includes Title I loans; see above.	Repayment time varies with the type of loan.

Doors and windows

Keep doors and windows firmly shut and locked to cut down heat loss in winter and heat gain in summer. Check your windows and door latches to see whether they fit tightly and, if necessary, adjust the latches and plug any air leaks. You don't really need to open windows in winter — you usually get enough fresh air just from normal air leakage even if your house is well caulked and weatherstripped.

Use heavy or insulated draperies, keep them closed at night, and fit them tightly at the top. In the summer and in warm climates, light colored curtains that you can't see through will reflect the sun and help keep your house cool.

The tightest storm door in the world doesn't work when it's open — try to cut down the number of times that you go in and out. Adding a vestibule at your front and back doors will also help to tighten up your house.

Attic and roof

Seal any openings between your attic and the rest of your house where air might escape, such as spaces around loosely-fitting attic stairway doors or pull-down stairways, penetrations of the ceiling for lights or a fan, and plumbing vents, pipes, or air ducts which pass into the attic — they don't seem like much, but they add up!

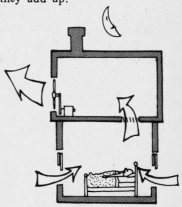

One alternative to energy-consuming air conditioning is the use of an *attic fan* to cool your home. Normally a house holds heat, so that there's a lag between the time the outside air cools after sunset on a summer night and the time that the house cools. The purpose of the attic fan is to speed up the cooling of the house by pulling air in through open windows up through the attic and out.

When the fan's on, you can let air through to the attic either by opening the attic door part way or by installing a louver that does the same thing automatically.

In a part of the country that has hot days and cool nights, using an attic fan in the evenings and closing the windows and curtains during the day can *replace* air conditioning. The *size* of the fan you buy should be determined by the amount of space you want to cool. You can figure out the fan size you need by finding the *volume* of your house: Rounding off to the nearest foot, multiply the length of your house by its width, then multiply by its height (from the ground to just below the attic). This will give you the volume in *cubic feet*. The capacity of all fans is marked on the fan in *CFM's* – *C*ubic *F*eet of air moved per *M*inute. Divide the volume of your house by 10; this will give you the CFM rating of the fan you need to change the air in the house 6 times an hour.

$$\underline{\hspace{3cm}} \div 10 = \underline{\hspace{3cm}}$$
volume of house   CFM fan rating

Basements

If you can't afford to insulate the exposed portions of your basement or crawl space for the winter, you can still create some barriers against wind and cold by planting shrubs around the foundation. You can also tarpaper the exposed walls and rake leaves against the foundation, covering them with a weighted tarp (the tarpaper keeps moisture off your house that would otherwise come in through the leaves.)

Shading your home

A good way to keep your house cool in the summer is to shade it from the outside. The east and west sides are where the most heat comes through – if you can shade here, it'll show up right away in a smaller air conditioning bill and a cooler home. Any way that stops the sun before it gets in through the

glass is *seven times* as good at keeping you cool as blinds and curtains on the inside. So trees and vines that shade in the summer and lose their leaves for the winter are what you want – they'll let the sun back in for the winter months. If you can't shade your house with trees, concentrate on keeping the sun out of your windows – awnings or even permanent sunshades will do the job (but only on the **south** side; they won't work on the east and west).

Hot water

See page 63 for hot water heater maintenance, and turn your heater down to 120° if you haven't already.

All your leaky faucets should be fixed – particularly the hot ones – one leaky faucet can waste up to 6000 gallons of water a year. You can also save by turning your water heater down when you'll be away from home for a weekend or more. Always use full loads in your dishwasher and clothes washer, and use warm wash and cold rinse. Take showers – they use less hot water than baths. You should use cold water to run your garbage disposal – in general, you *save* every time you use cold water instead of hot.

Heating

(See Part 3 for the details on how to keep your system tuned)

In Part 2 (page 25), you can figure out how much you can save by lowering your thermostat. For an extra investment of about $80, you can install a clock thermostat, which will automatically turn your heat down every night and turn it up in the morning. Something that'll do the same job for about $40 is a time-delay thermostat, which is a wind-up timer wired into your thermostat.

More efficient oil burners are available now. If you have oil heating, you can check with your oil company about the new high-speed flame-retention oil burners — they can save you 10% on you oil bill.

Your furnace may be too big. If your house has been insulated since it was built, then your furnace may be too big for your home. In general that means it's inefficient, and would use less fuel overall if it were smaller. Here's how to tell: wait for one of the coldest nights of the year, and set your thermostat at 70°. Once the house temperature reaches 70°, if the furnace burner runs *less* than 40 minutes out of the next hour (time it only when it's running), your furnace is too big. A furnace that's too big turns on and off much more than it should, and that wastes energy. Call your service company — depending on your type of fuel burner, they may be able to cut down the size of your burner without replacing it.

Don't overheat rooms and don't heat or cool rooms you're not using. It's important that no room in your house get more heating than it needs, and that you should be able to turn down the heating or cooling in areas of your home that you don't use. If

some of your rooms get too hot before the other rooms are warm enough, you're paying for fuel you don't need, and your system needs *balancing* — call your serviceman. If your house is "zoned," you've got more than one thermostat and can turn down heating or cooling in areas where they're not needed.

But if your house has only one thermostat, you can't properly adjust the temperature in rooms you're not using, and that wastes energy too. You can correct this situation fairly cheaply — try these steps on your system:

Steam Radiators — most valves on radiators are all-on or all-off, but you can buy valves that let you set any temperature you like for that radiator.

Forced-Air Heating or Cooling — Many registers (the place where the air comes out) are adjustable. If not, get ones that are, so you can balance your system.

Hot-water Radiators — if there are valves on your radiators at all, you can use them to adjust the temperature room by room.

Air conditioning

Controlling your air conditioner's thermostat is discussed in detail in Part 2 (see page 25). Closing off unused rooms is just as important in saving on air conditioning as it is for heating. Keep lights off during the day — most of the electricity they use makes heat, not light. You can also reduce the load on your air conditioning system by not using heat-generating appliances like your dishwasher during the hot part of the day (or stop the dishwasher when the drying cycle begins).

If you have central air conditioning, you may want to look into the *air economizer,* a system which turns off the part of your air conditioner that uses a lot of electricity, and circulates outside air through the house when it's cooler out than it is in. By using the cooler outside air, the system reduces its own job and saves money for you. Ask your air conditioning dealer if he can install one on your system.

Buying a room air conditioner

When you go to buy a room air conditioning unit, check the EER — Energy Efficiency Ratio. The higher the EER number, the less electricity the unit will use to cool the same amount of air — you should con-

JUST THE HIGH E.E.R. MODELS, PLEASE

sider your possible fuel savings when deciding how much to spend on your air conditioning unit. A unit which costs more to begin with may save enough money over the next summer to make it worth it.

Typical EER's available range from 4 to 12; a unit with an EER of 4 will cost about **3 times as much** to operate as one with an EER of 12.

The heat pump

A heat pump runs on electricity, and is just like an air conditioner, except it can run in reverse — it can use electricity to heat, and gets more heat out of a dollar's worth of electricity than the resistance heaters in baseboard units and electric furnaces.

How? — there's heat in the air outside your home, even when the temperature's below freezing, and a heat pump can get that warmth out and into your house. When should you consider installing one? — If you presently have a central electric heating system, and live south of Pennsylvania, it may pay to install a heat pump in the system, next to the furnace. Keep your electric furnace — once the temperature drops below 20° or so, the heat pump will need help from the furnace. Installation of a heat pump large enough for most houses should cost a little under $3000, but you're getting central air conditioning as well as a "furnace" that's about 1½ times more efficient than your electric furnace.

If you're adding a room, consider adding a heat pump — like air conditioners they come in room size units. A heat pump for a room comes with its own electric resistance coil (like a baseboard electric heater) for the times of the year when it's too cold for the heat pump itself to work well. Call your air conditioner dealer for details on both central and room-size heat pumps. If your furnace runs on gas or oil, and the prices of those fuels continue to rise faster than the price of electricity, then you'll want to consider a heat pump too.

Heating water with your air conditioner

The part of the whole-house air conditioner that sits outside your house gives off a tremendous amount of heat. If your house is centrally air conditioned and you live far enough south so that your system runs more than 3 months out of the year, there's a way to use the energy the air-conditioner gives off to heat your domestic hot water. A simple device is fitted to your air conditioner, and pipes run from your water heater. The installed cost of this is significant, but you get it back over time in free hot water that is heated by your air conditioner. Call your electric company or an air conditioning repairman to see if this energy saver is available in your area.

Lights

Plan your lighting sensibly — reduce lighting where possible, concentrating it in work areas or reading areas where it is really needed. Fluorescent bulbs should be used rather than the incandescent kind.

A 25-watt fluorescent bulb gives off as much light as a 100-watt incandescent bulb, but costs one fourth as much to light. Decorative gas lanterns should be turned off or converted to electric lamps — they will use much less energy to produce the same amount of light.

Energy from the sun

Ways to heat and cool your house that use the sun's energy are available *now*. The parts of the system are simple — a large flat panel called a *collector* sits on the roof of your house or on the ground next to it. The collector is about half the size of your roof, faces south, and is tilted at roughly 45 degrees. That's in the northern U.S. — the further south, the flatter the collector.

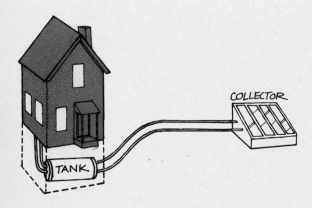

In the collector, the sun heats up either air or a water-antifreeze mixture that takes the heat into a *storage tank*. The tank, which is usually filled with water, needs to hold about 2,000 gallons. This tank can also be filled with rocks (a slightly larger tank is required) — in that case heated air from the collector brings the heat to the tank. The storage tank is then used as a source of heat for your home heating system, either a slightly changed forced air or hot water system, or one especially installed for the purpose. In the summer, using what's called an *absorption* air conditioning system, your house can be cooled using that same heat. The cost for a solar heating system for an average house runs $3000-$5000 for a new house and varies greatly for existing houses, but is virtually free from operating cost compared to the system you have now.

What about nights and cloudy days? A solar heating system is never intended to fulfill *all* the heating needs of a house — the storage tank carries enough heat to get through a few overcast days and nights, after that your normal system must carry the load. As the cost of fuel rises, solar heating and cooling will make more and more sense: In 1974, a solar system paid for itself in a little more than 10 years — if fuel costs continue to go up, that time will get shorter.

Energy from the wind

Windmills that pump water and generate electricity have been around a long time. Recently 2 things are happening that make using a wind generator attractive as a generator for your home: first, windmills and the batteries for the electricity they store are getting more efficient — a modern windmill can grab and hold more electricity out of the same amount of wind. Second, the cost of your monthly electric bill is going up and once a windmill's installed, electricity is nearly free. Like solar heating, a windmill isn't designed to generate *all* your needs — you still need a standard source of electricity — but except for houses with electric heat, a wind generator will give you plenty of electricity, and pay for itself in less than 10 years.

New ways to get back waste heat

A lot of the fuel you buy to heat your house is wasted — it goes up your chimney, and it goes up your chimney whether your furnace is running or not. There are 2 energy-saving devices coming that can grab that heat before it gets out. (**Note:** if you have electric heat these don't apply. Also, neither of these devices is presently approved for use, but they are coming soon.)

1. **The heatpipe** — this is a small pipe that is installed to sit in the stream of hot flue gases running from your furnace to your chimney. The pipe is very good at conducting heat, and it does just that, taking heat out of the flue gas and moving it a short distance — usually into a warm air duct. So instead of going up the chimney the heat stays in your house.

2. **The motorized flue damper** — you know that if you leave your fireplace damper open when there's no fire going, a lot of warm air that you've paid to heat goes up the chimney — this same thing happens with your furnace when it's not running. A motorized flue damper works just like the one in your fireplace, except it's automatic — when the furnace is running, the damper's open, and the instant the furnace shuts off the damper closes.

DIRECTIONS

THESE ARE THE TWO PAGES THAT PUT IT ALL TOGETHER. YOU ALREADY KNOW FROM PART 2 WHICH OF THESE LINES YOU WANT TO COMPLETE. HERE'S HOW TO FINISH THEM.

To fill in lines 1-5:

First, use Part 2 to fill in the Cost and Savings Factor for each line you're interested in.

Lines 2 and 4:

Get your Heating Factor from page 28 and fill it into the oval (○) on lines 2 and 4. Find your yearly dollar savings like this:

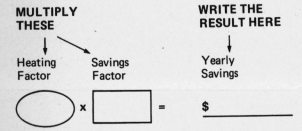

MULTIPLY THESE → Heating Factor, Savings Factor

WRITE THE RESULT HERE → Yearly Savings

Lines 1, 3, and 5:

Get your Heating Factor from page 28 and fill it into the Heating Factor oval (○).

If you **do** have whole-house air conditioning, get your Cooling Factor from page 28 and fill it into the oval (○).

If you **don't** have whole-house air conditioning, put zeros into the Cooling Factor oval, like this: (○).

Get your yearly dollar savings like this:

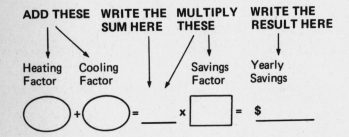

ADD THESE → Heating Factor, Cooling Factor

WRITE THE SUM HERE

MULTIPLY THESE → Savings Factor

WRITE THE RESULT HERE → Yearly Savings

How to fill in lines 6, 7, and 8:

Just copy your yearly savings from pages 25, 26, and 27 into the appropriate boxes on the checklist.

WHAT ARE YOUR BEST INVESTMENTS?

There are two kinds of investments here — the kind you have to make each year, and the kind you only have to make once. Here's how to directly compare the two different kinds of investments and figure out which are your best bets:

For the investments that you have to make each year (lines 2a, 2b, 7, and 8), use this method: simply subtract the yearly cost from the yearly savings, and write the difference in the right-hand box on the line of the checklist dealing with the measure. This number is the net savings per year for the investment.

$$\underline{\qquad}_{\text{savings}} - \underline{\qquad}_{\text{cost}} = \underline{\qquad}_{\text{net savings}}$$

For "one-shot" investments that you only have to pay for once (lines 1, 2c, 3-5), multiply the yearly savings by 13, subtract the cost from the result, and write the difference in the right-hand box on the line of the checklist dealing with the measure. This number is the net savings over the life of the investment.

$$\underline{\qquad}_{\text{(savings x 13*)}} - \underline{\qquad}_{\text{cost}} = \underline{\qquad}_{\text{net savings}}$$

*Multiplying your estimated savings in the first year by 13 projects the savings (in terms of today's money) that a "one-shot" energy-saving improvement will deliver to you over its life. The figure 13 takes into account the rate of inflation, and assumes that you can borrow money at the average available interest rate.

HOW TO INTERPRET THE CHECKLIST

Now you're ready to figure out what are the best energy-savings steps for you.

First — look at the cost figures. Don't consider doing things you can't afford. But be sure you don't leave out things you **can** afford — read page 64, which tells you how to finance home improvements.

Second — for the measures you can afford, look at the net savings in the right-hand column. The things to do first are the things that have the highest net savings. Do the measures with the highest net savings, then the next highest, and so on — until you've done all you can afford. Don't do a measure if the net savings are less than 0.

Now you're ready to go on to part 3 — the "How-to" part. It starts on page 31.

ENERGY CHECKLIST

	SAVINGS FACTOR FROM PART 2	YEARLY SAVINGS	COST FROM PART 2	NET SAVINGS

1. CAULK AND WEATHERSTRIP

Heating factor + Cooling factor = _____ × [Savings factor] = $ _____   Total cost $ [ ]   [ ]

2. ADD STORM WINDOWS

a) plastic storm windows
(with no new weatherstripping)

Heating factor × [Savings factor] = $ _____   Yearly cost $ [ ]   [ ]

b) plastic storm windows
(with new weatherstripping — be sure to fill out line 1 above)

Heating factor × [Savings factor] = $ _____   Yearly cost $ [ ]   [ ]

c) glass storm windows
(with new weatherstripping — be sure to fill out line 1 above)

Heating factor × [Savings factor] = $ _____   Total cost $ [ ]   [ ]

3. INSULATE ATTIC

Fill out both lines if your attic is a combination of two basic attic types (see page 11). Otherwise, fill out the top line only.

Heating factor + Cooling factor = _____ × [Savings factor] = $ _____   Total cost $ [ ]   [ ]

Heating factor + Cooling factor = _____ × [Savings factor] = $ _____   Total cost $ [ ]   [ ]

4. FILL OUT THE LINE OR LINES THAT APPLY TO YOU.

a) Insulate crawl space walls

Heating factor × [Savings factor] = $ _____   Total cost $ [ ]   [ ]

b) Insulate floor

Heating factor × [Savings factor] = $ _____   Total cost $ [ ]   [ ]

c) Insulate basement walls

Heating factor × [Savings factor] = $ _____   Total cost $ [ ]   [ ]

5. INSULATE FRAME WALLS

Heating factor + Cooling factor = _____ × [Savings factor] = $ _____   Total cost $ [ ]   [ ]

6. REGULATE THERMOSTAT
Down in winter, up in summer.

Degrees turndown [ ]   From Part 2 $ [ ]   Yearly cost $ 0   [ ]

7. SERVICE OIL OR COAL-BURNING FURNACE

From Part 2 $ [ ]   Yearly cost $ 25-30   [ ]

8. SERVICE WHOLE-HOUSE AIR CONDITIONER

From Part 2 $ [ ]   Yearly cost $ 25-30   [ ]

Index